# MODEL BEHAVIOUR

## teresa maughan

photography by sean pollock
and james meaneaux stenson

First published in 2001 by Channel 4 Books, an imprint of Pan Macmillan Ltd,
20 New Wharf Road, London N1 9RR, Basingstoke and Oxford.

Associated companies throughout the world.

www.panmacmillan.com

ISBN 0 7522 6187 8

Text © Channel 4 Books, 2001

Front cover photograph © Sean Pollock, 2001
Back cover photographs © James Meaneaux Stenson, 2001

9 8 7 6 5 4 3 2 1

A CIP catalogue record for this book is available from the British Library.

Designed by seagulls
Printed by Bath Press

Picture credits: pp6-45 James Meaneaux Stenson; pp62-73 Donna Francesca;
pp52-57, 74-95 Sean Pollock; p96 Carlo Dalla Chiesa

This book accompanies the television series *Model Behaviour*,
made by Princess Productions for Channel 4.

*Executive Producer:* Henrietta Conrad
*Series Producer:* Justin Gorman
*Producer:* Madeleine Knight

# contents

# MODEL BEHAVIOUR

# introduction

Are you ready for a roller-coaster ride to find the face of 2001 with Channel 4's *Model Behaviour*? Follow nearly 5,000 wannabe models battle it out in a series of gruelling auditions and interviews, to be one of twenty-one lucky girls who will travel to London for a model workshop week, where the final selection process begins...

Commiserate with the eleven young hopefuls who will be rejected after just two days, and congratulate the shortlist of ten who make it to the end of the week. Experience their embarrassment and their triumph as they master the catwalk, pose in front of a leading fashion photographer and have a complete makeover. After all that, just five will be moving into an apartment in London and getting the chance to change their lives forever.

The programme follows the final five's progress over four months – witness the tears, the tantrums, the highs and lows, the joy and the sorrow as the girls struggle to learn the modelling ropes and come to terms with living with each other under the ever-present eye of the cameras. Watch them as they discover what life is really like for a model taking her first steps into the competitive world of fashion...

All five compete to win the coveted prize of a contract with leading agency Premier Model Management and the once-in-a-lifetime chance to be on the cover of *Cosmopolitan*. As the tension rises and the competition intensifies, two girls are chosen to take part in London Fashion Week. And which one will win through to take away the ultimate prize? That would be telling!

# *the* auditions

Over 4,500 girls from six different cities around the United Kingdom and Ireland have one thing in common – they all want to be the next Kate Moss or Claudia Schiffer. *Model Behaviour* gives them the chance to make their dreams come true in a unique competition to find a supermodel. The *MB* panel of judges – Angus Munro, Head Booker at London's Premier Model Management, Lorraine Candy, Editor-in-Chief of *Cosmopolitan*, and Oliver Woods, hairstylist to the stars including Kate Moss and Jude Law – is about to put the girls through a gruelling selection process that will whittle the thousands of wannabes down to only a handful of finalists. But who will be the lucky ones, and who will be the losers?

We begin at the open auditions in Birmingham, where 600 young hopefuls gather in the city centre, all with dreams of becoming the next big thing...

The judges: Oliver Woods, Lorraine Candy and Angus Munro.

## BIRMINGHAM - Day One
### Grand Moathouse Hotel

**6.00am** All over the Midlands, girls between the ages of sixteen and twenty-four roll out of bed, put on their make-up and psych themselves up to enter a competition that could change their lives – *Model Behaviour*.

**7.30am** At Birmingham's Grand Moathouse Hotel the queue is already halfway down the road as young hopefuls gather in anticipation. First in the queue is twenty-one-year old Barbara, who is there because she reckons she has what it takes to be a successful model. But will the judges agree?

**9.00am** The doors open and there is a rush of girls as auditioning finally begins. To avoid a stampede, the girls are invited through in groups of sixty to be registered. Any under the age of eighteen must have a signed permission form from their parents – if they don't, they are asked to leave.

**9.15am** The first line-up of ten girls is called forward to strut its stuff in front of Angus, Lorraine and Ollie, not to mention the camera crew and TV production staff. First up is Barbara, who walks confidently up and down and stops to chat to the judges. When asked if she thinks she is model material, she replies, 'You've got to be in it to win it.'

Over 4,500 girls queued up to
attend the six nation-wide auditions.

**10.00am** Sixth in line is a tall, slender young girl called Jessica and she immediately catches the attention of the judges. Jessica is sixteen today and is therefore just eligible to take part; but will her birthday end up being a happy one?

**10.34am** Jessica gets the best birthday prezzie ever – news that she's got through to day two. Barbara isn't as lucky, but she's cool about it: 'If you don't get picked it's no big deal.' With an average of only one out of twenty girls being selected, Barbara isn't alone.

**12.30pm** Girls are still arriving thick and fast; many have been waiting for several hours to get the chance to shine. The judges have already assessed over 270 girls, but despite having been hard at it for over three hours, they still eagerly await the next new line-up to walk the makeshift catwalk. They might select one or two girls from each group... on the other hand, maybe no one will be lucky.

**Lunchtime** The Panel gets a much-needed breather to grab a sandwich and reflect on the girls seen so far. The judges are all looking for beautiful girls, but they don't always agree on what exactly that means. Angus is looking for, 'Someone I call a crossover girl. Someone who can do the editorial for magazines like *Vogue* and big advertising campaigns for, say, Prada or Gucci, as well as catalogue work.' Oliver, on the other hand, is looking for an out-of-the-ordinary style: 'I am not looking for someone who is conventionally drop-dead gorgeous, but for a girl with a more "street" look.' As Editor-in-Chief of Britain's leading women's magazine, Lorraine Candy has different criteria again: 'I'm looking for a cover girl who is really sexy, really pretty and really glamorous. She mustn't be too edgy or alienate our readers.'

**'It was the hardest decision, who to pick. You have to go with your instincts at the time.'**
*Oliver Woods, Judge*

**2.00pm** It's the first line-up of the afternoon and tensions are mounting. Even the panel can't agree on which girls to choose from, and arguments break out between Oliver and Angus. Ollie wants to choose Chantel, aged eighteen, but Angus cannot understand why, and insists they should take Amelia, nineteen. Eventually the two panellists agree to disagree and both girls get through.

**2.30pm** So far the judges have seen over 420 girls, including Christie, seventeen, who 'wants to be really, really famous', whether it be as a model, actress, athlete or pop star, and Nyathesis, nineteen, who has

The Panel don't always agree on who should get through...

Sophie has a last minute glance in the mirror to make sure she's looking her best.

## BIRMINGHAM – Day Two
### Grand Moathouse Hotel

**9.00am** Twenty girls return for the second selection day, from which only three or four of the girls will go through to the workshop week in London. Lorraine briefs the twenty hopefuls, explaining that within an hour and a half, some of the girls will be leaving. 'It's up to you to prove to us that you've got what it takes to be a supermodel,' she tells them.

**9.30am** The girls line up to walk a 7-metre red carpet so the judges can assess each of them on their looks, their walk and their confidence.

**10.00am** Lorraine, Ollie and Angus then go away to another room to discuss each of the entrants in turn, leaving the girls themselves to wait anxiously.

**10.30am** The panel emerges from its huddle and Ollie asks the twenty girls to walk left or right of him, so as to form two groups. He then announces which group is staying and which will, sadly, have to go. Seven girls make it through, including Sophie, Nyathesis and Jessica. Thirteen tearful wannabes are left behind, their dreams of being a model having been brought to an abrupt end.

**11.00am** The lucky seven are then asked to remove all traces of make-up so the judges can see their skin. 'A cover girl's skin is very important,' explains Lorraine, 'as photographers will often come in really close to the face.'

**12.00pm** The girls are then asked to change into black shorts with a matching top. Each of the girls is asked to

bags of personality and confidence. But which, if any, of the girls will make it to the next round?

**6.30pm** The last girls are tired and hungry but still eager to get their chance to impress the judges. Each girl who is chosen from the line-up of ten receive either a green sticker (definite model potential) or a red sticker (possible model potential). So far, only nineteen girls have been selected out of 590.

**7.05pm** It's the last line-up of the day and the judges are excited by a girl called Sophie, sixteen, whom they think is a real find. Unsurprisingly, Sophie gets a green sticker, 'That was so very, very scary. I really didn't expect to be picked,' she wails. Lorraine couldn't be more enthusiastic about her: 'Sophie has striking looks with a personality to match.'

Dressed in matching black top and shorts, the girls parade before the judges.

walk the catwalk again – all bare-faced and dressed the same so that the judges can make the final selection.

**2.30pm** They are then interviewed in turn so the panel can get a feel for their personalities and for whether they've got the right qualities to succeed in the competitive world of modelling.

**5.00pm** Finally, the judges retire to have a discussion about who should go through to the next stage. Will it be confident Nyathesis? Or level-headed Stacey, aged nineteen? Or maybe twenty-year-old Adeela, who has just moved in with her forty-three-year-old boyfriend? The girls wait nervously to find out whether they'll be going to London... Adeela worries that she won't be: 'I don't know what I'll do if I don't get through.'

**5.20pm** The waiting is over. Ollie tells the girls to stand up if their number is called.

**5.30pm** Four very happy and excited girls hug each other as they prepare to travel to London in a few days' time for the second stage of the competition. They are Sophie, Nyathesis, Jessica and Vicky. A tearful Adeela sobs that, 'It's all been for nothing.' Of 600 girls, only four have made it through to the next stage – and that will be even more gruelling and competitive than the experience they've just undergone.

Stacey gets her chance to impress.

Alicia from Sheffield queuing at the Manchester auditions.

## MANCHESTER - Day One
### Dancehouse Theatre

**8.00am** In Manchester, there has been an amazing response: over 700 teenagers have turned out to try and make their mark as a model.

**9.00am** The theatre doors open and the first girls go in, leaving another 630 waiting in the queue. These include Rokshaneh, eighteen, who reveals that none of the clothes she's standing up in are hers: 'I normally wear baggy stuff, but I thought I'd go a bit glitzy and glam today,' she confides. 'My feet are killing me in these sandals, though!'

**10.05am** The judges are impressed by Rokshaneh's bubbly personality as she gleefully announces, 'I feel like a right slapper in these clothes.' Like most of the other girls, however, she also has blisters and is hot and tired.

**10.15am** Rokshaneh isn't called back, as the judges don't feel she is right. Fed up, she gives them a piece of her mind: 'You know exactly what the winner will look like in the end – really skinny and tall.'

**Lunchtime** Typically, the Manchester weather is cold and drizzly as 300 girls still queue outside, waiting to be seen. Eighteen-year-old Alicia, from Sheffield, is one of them: 'I've never wanted to be a model,' she admits. 'My friend Jo persuaded me to come.'

**2.30pm** The first afternoon line-up includes Rebecca, nineteen, who has come with her mum, and Annabel, who's a ballet dancer and only 5'5". Annabel is soon delighted to hear that she's been picked to come back tomorrow, while Rebecca and her mother leave disappointed.

**4.30pm** Many of the girls have come with portfolios,

'At the auditions I was very much not bothered. If I hadn't got through, it wouldn't have broken my heart.'
*Alicia, Manchester*

Annabel made it through the first day of auditions, and couldn't wait to share the news with her family.

including twenty-three-year-old Lindsay, who is auditioning because her grandma, who died earlier in the year, always wanted her granddaughter to try to become a model. But Lindsay doesn't get the call-back she was hoping for.

**6.30pm** It's getting late and the girls are getting tired. Some have been waiting for over six hours, including Alicia, who finally gets to strut her stuff. 'By the time I got in there I was hot, and tired. My nose was running, my head was thumping and my face was bright red and I walked up and down thinking, "Oh my God, why am I doing this?"'

**6.40pm** The competition is intense, and the judges are impressed at the quality of all the girls in Alicia's line-up. After a few minutes of deliberation, they decide to take three girls — Alicia, Patricia and Kim — through to day two.

**8.30pm** It's the end of a long and emotional day. Only twenty-two girls have been recalled for day two,

leaving 678 unhappy wannabes to go home to commiserations from their friends and families.

## MANCHESTER - Day Two
### Dancehouse Theatre

**9.00am** Nerves are jangling as the twenty-two girls return for day two of the selection process. Having got this far makes the girls more anxious about the prospects of getting through. Knowing that over half will be leaving in less than an hour makes them both excited and jittery.

**10.00am** Each potential model walks the red carpet, which acts as catwalk, hopeful of getting the judges' attention. Alicia actually feels guilty about getting this far: 'People here yesterday really, really wanted to be a model and I just wanted to give up and go home.'

**10.30am** There are tears of joy and tears of sorrow as the girls are told who is going home and who is staying on. Annabel is not surprised to hear she's one of the unlucky ones – 'I guessed I wouldn't get through,' she says. Lara, sixteen, can't believe her luck, 'I didn't imagine I would be picked.' Alicia on the other hand isn't at all fazed. 'I think I've got what it takes to go all the way,' she says, confidently.

> **'Think about being a model before you get into it. Have a long, long think – take everything with a pinch of salt.'**
> *Alicia, Manchester*

**11.00am** As with the Birmingham auditions, the girls must now bare all, by removing their make-up and changing into the matching shorts and tops that have been selected for them. Not everybody is happy with the prospect. 'I don't want to do it in front of the cameras,' says a worried Christina, aged sixteen.

**11.20am** The judges go down the line of eager young hopefuls one by one, scrutinizing their naked faces.

**12.00am** It's time for the catwalk. Some of the girls will try anything to stand out from the crowd. It's important for the judges to see that the girls have 'body confidence' as well as great looks and personality. Christina, despite being nervous, has a great walk and the judges are impressed.

**2.10pm** Interviews begin and the girls reveal a little more of their personalities. 'I really, really want this,' admits Lara. Alicia remains cool and admits that she can be a bit 'mardy' – something the judges have already noticed.

**3.20pm** If Samantha gets picked to go to London, she'll have a difficult choice to make. She has already been invited to enter another model competition in Brazil... which will she choose?

**4.00pm** Decision time, and the judges are finding it tricky to narrow down the final four. 'Cayte has a brilliant smile...', 'Christina has a good body but her face lacks definition...', 'Alicia is a sexy model'. (Ollie thinks Alicia is 'shot-putter sexy', however.) So who will be going through to the next stage?

**5.10pm** The *Model Behaviour* panel has come to a decision and announces the names of the final four – Alicia, Lara, Samantha and Sarah. The girls are overjoyed but sad for the six who didn't get picked... Now Samantha has a choice to make: will it be London or Brazil?

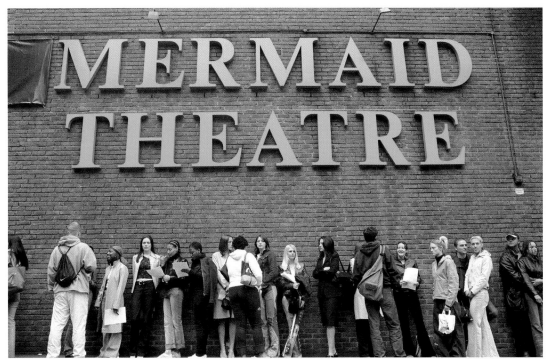

The Mermaid Theatre played host to the biggest model auditions ever held in London.

## LONDON – Day One
### Mermaid Theatre

**8.30am** Despite the bleak weather, over 800 girls wait patiently outside the Mermaid Theatre in Blackfriars, London. Zoe, who has wanted to be a model since she was a child, got here at 5.45am: 'I got up at 2.00am to get here and I'm first in the queue.' Patricia is queuing with her sister, but isn't keen to be there: 'I've been in the queue for six hours in the rain and every hour I say I'm going home, but my sister and my friend won't let me.'

**9.00am** The doors open and the first sixty girls head for the registration desk – and then for the toilets, to have a last glance in the mirror.

> **'The worst thing about the auditions was waiting. Once I was in there it was 8.00pm, so I didn't get home until 11.30pm.'**
> *Elizabeth, London*

**10.05am** The judges have gone through two lines already and have seen Karen, who apart from having a bubbly personality can also jump into the splits. She is only 4'11", though, something that may hinder her chances of getting through. Rebecca comes to the attention of the judges, both because of her attractive looks and slim frame, but also because of her larger-

Seventeen year-old Patricia queues for hours to be seen. Will it be worth the wait?

Through to the second round!

CONGRATULATIONS

YOU HAVE MADE IT THROUGH TO THE
SECOND ROUND OF
MODEL BEHAVIOUR

than-life personality. She has already decided to call herself Sexy Becks, but will she sway the judges?

**10.20am** Rebecca's outgoing personality earns her a call-back to the next day. Karen isn't so lucky and isn't chosen, but at least she's demonstrated how good-natured she is: 'I didn't have many friends at school but I want to prove I can do it and I'm a nice person.'

**11.00am** The toilets are heaving with girls making last-minute applications of lip gloss and mascara and adjusting stray hairs and bra straps. Security can only allow a few girls in at once, and for a set period only – otherwise there'd be a riot. Mirror time is a precious commodity.

**11.20am** Already the judges have seen several line-ups. With only twenty girls likely to get through to day two, over ninety-five per cent will be given a knock-back. But will they all be able to cope with the disappointment?

**'On the second day I had to be dragged there. I felt really sick on the train up there – just knowing I had to go back and do it again.'**
*Patricia, London*

**12.25pm** Not everyone is happy with the judges' decisions, including Anita (twenty-four), who hasn't been picked. 'You are just looking for someone who looks like they've been dead and buried,' she complains. 'I'll come looking like a tramp next time.'

**2.10pm** Tempers are frayed. Everyone is tired, and some girls just have to get their frustrations off their chest. Twenty-four-year-old Tiffany is fed up with the whole selection process and makes sure the panel knows about it: 'It's obvious you are looking for a certain type of person, which eliminates most of us straight away because we're not what you want,' she grumbles. 'You could have saved us a seven-hour wait in a queue by telling us that in the first place.' Ollie and Angus feel that every girl has a chance, whatever her look, but Tiffany doesn't see it his way. Angus explains the model criteria and Tiffany agrees to disagree.

**4.00pm** Ollie, Angus and Lorraine have seen over 400 girls. Every member of the panel is now beginning to feel extremely tired. However, despite their weariness, they are

The heartbreaking wait for a callback.

It's hard work behind the scenes too.

determined to give each girl the same chance to shine, including Lucia who says that she 'wants to be the next Caprice'.

**7.00pm** It's getting late, but the judges have still only seen 700 girls and there are another 300 waiting to come in and show off their assets. Twenty have been recalled for day two already.

**7.20pm** It's one of the last line-ups of the day, and the judges are very excited about one particular girl – Chermaine, aged seventeen, whom they think has got all the right qualities to be a model. 'She's got an exceptional look, a great body and a great personality. She's the jewel in the crown as far as I'm concerned,' enthuses Ollie. At 5'8", Chermaine has the height too.

**8.30pm** It's been a long and emotional day. The judges have had to cope with tears and tantrums and humiliation and rejection, but they have now selected thirty girls who will be coming back to do it all again tomorrow...

## LONDON – Day Two
### Mermaid Theatre

**9.00am** Chermaine, Esther and Abi are just three of the lucky girls who were recalled – and they're ecstatic. 'I

Patricia takes to the floor.

got through,' Chermaine exclaims joyously, 'can you believe it?' Angus explains that it's now up to them to show the judges that they have what it takes to go all the way – otherwise they'll be going home in under an hour and a half.

**10.00am** Thirty girls have to walk up and down the red carpet to give the judges a glimpse of their potential modelling ability.

**10.30am** It's decision time. For Abi, waiting to hear whether she is going to stay on for the rest of the day is nearly unbearable. It falls to the judges to split the hopefuls into two groups – Abi is in one and Chermaine is in another – and let them know which group is out of the competition.

**10.40am** It isn't the news Abi had been hoping for. Devastated, she leaves the auditorium immediately. 'I'm not going to give up, though,' she sobs.

Chermaine is through, however – and understandably euphoric. 'We are so lucky to be here,' she gushes, 'It's amazing.'

**11.00am** The next hurdle that the ten victors face is to be in front of the cameras without a scrap of make-up on. For Patricia, aged seventeen, this will be particularly difficult, as she has a bad skin condition. She is worried that once the panel sees her complexion she'll be ruled out of the competition.

**11.10am** Lorraine asks the make-up free girls to line up and she walks up and down them. Seeing Patricia's obvious discomfort at having to show her skin to all the other girls on camera, she doesn't single her out in the line.

**11.30am** With the worst bit over as far as Patricia is concerned, the ten finalists have to strip off their own clothes and put on the two-piece selected for them.

Not all of the girls are happy about this part of the selection process, though. 'I hate having to wear the black shorts and top because I know I have got really big thighs,' reveals Patricia. Elizabeth isn't happy at the prospect either: 'I initially thought "Oh my God" when I saw the black two-piece we had to wear, and then I thought, "It's not as if they are asking us to strip naked..."'

**2.00pm** With the catwalk over, it's on to the final selection process – the one-on-three interviews. Each girl has a different reason for entering the competition. 'I've never done anything like this before,' explains Cari, aged seventeen, 'but I've loved very minute of it.' Chermaine explains, 'I want to be a model because it's

## 'I thought the auditions were the best part because they were fun and quite exciting.'
### Chermaine, London

Elizabeth and Chermaine go through the process.

every girl's dream.' Sadly, it's a dream that won't come true for at least six of these remaining ten girls; but which will it be?

**4.00pm** For some, getting through is not necessarily a good thing. 'You don't want to get through because you know it will be harder when they say, "Sorry, you're not through,"' comments seventeen-year-old Kalee.

**6.00pm** After waiting for an agonizing two hours for the judges' decision, the girls are all desperate to find out if they will be going to London for the workshop week. But what did the judges think of them?

'Natalie had a great symmetry to her face, great figure and a good personality, but something's not quite right,' says Angus, noting also that, 'Patricia has the best face out of all of them, but she does have bad skin.' 'Of all the girls we've seen, perhaps Patricia would be transformed the most. She's definitely my favourite,' comments Lorraine. 'I think Becky has such an unusual face,' she continues, 'but for what I'm looking for, she is wrong.'

**6.30pm** All is about to be revealed by Angus. He tells the assembled girls that they've all got what it takes to be a model, but that only four will have the chance to prove it in London. After much deliberation, the judges have decided to call back Patricia, Elizabeth, Sexy Becks and Chermaine. A disappointed Natalie observes that, 'One of the girls' complexions, doesn't look that clear to me. Maybe they are hoping it clears up.' So it's all been worth it for Patricia: 'When I was selected I just couldn't believe it. Now I am pleased that I did so well and got through.'

Auditions in Dublin take place at The Temple Theatre, while in Edinburgh the venue is The Hibernian Football Club. Only two girls from each venue are through. From Dublin, the panel chooses nineteen-year-old Rowena, who is thrilled to be picked, and Sita, aged twenty-four, who's a little more laid-back: 'Whatever happens, happens,' she comments, philosophically. In Scotland the two lucky winners are Rose, aged eighteen, who is confident she will be the next Kate Moss, and Lisa, aged sixteen, who has one very clear aim: 'I just want to be famous.' There is only one more venue to visit and four more places up for grabs to go on the workshop week in London – stage two of the competition.

Three Dublin hopefuls plead their case.

## BRISTOL – Day One
### Marriott Hotel

**7.45am** A crowd is already gathering outside the Marriott Hotel and the atmosphere is buzzing. So far, the judges have auditioned more than 3,500 girls and the competition has been intense. The judges themselves have been bowled over by the quality and standard of all the girls that have auditioned, as Lorraine reveals: 'I was astonished by their confidence. They were all amazingly confident women of sixteen to eighteen, who were really able to carry themselves, really focused on what they wanted out of life, really clever mature women – and that filled me with joy.'

**9.00am** Time for the first sixty girls to enter the audition, including nineteen-year-old Elizabeth, who says all her friends say she should model; Gemma, aged seventeen, who reveals, 'My mum reckons I've got a model look'; and nineteen-year-old Emma, who admits she has wanted to be a model since she was very young and has already spent over £600 on portfolio pictures and agency fees. Angus emphasizes that you shouldn't pay an agency to put you on its books – if they like you, they will sign you free of charge.

**10.00am** One of the first girls through the doors is Donna, aged twenty, who feels this will be her last attempt at getting into the world of fashion modelling. 'Topless modelling seems the only thing open to me because of the way I am built, but I'm going to give it [fashion modelling] one more try.' In the same line-up is sixteen-year-old Alexandria, who is pretty but quite reserved. The judges have made their decision – Donna is leaving and Alexandria is through to the next round. Donna doesn't seem surprised by the result – 'I'll stick to taking my top off.'

**12.00pm** While Donna is resigned to glamour modelling, Tracey, aged twenty-four, feels it's time to get out of it, commenting, 'I really want to do better work and get treated better.' The judges then spy Layla, a dark-skinned nineteen-year-old who is over 6ft tall. Ollie is impressed: 'She has a great body.' Layla gets through to day two. Tracey, however, doesn't.

**2.45pm** Line after line of girls are seen by the judges... sometimes they don't choose anybody at all...

**4.00pm** It's the penultimate line-up of the day and so far the judges have called back seventeen girls. This is the best they've seen all day and three girls in particular grab their attention – nineteen-year-old Jenny Davies, all dressed in black, is very attractive but lacks height. Lorraine points out that she has beautiful skin, almost like porcelain, and the rest of the panel agree that she's in with a chance. Jenny Richards has come with her boyfriend Craig; by rights, they should be heading off for a holiday in Torquay. 'I thought we'd be finished and on our way by now,' Jenny reveals. Ollie and Angus are both made up that they've seen Jenny –

**'The worst bit was when there were loads of us and they divided us into two groups and they said, "Right ,you stand to the left and you to the right," and all the people on the right were thinking, "Oh my God, I think it's them that got through." We were standing nearest the door, so we thought we were going to get kicked out. When we got through, we were so relieved.'**
*Jenny, Bristol*

'She's fantastic!' Lorraine, however, doesn't think she is cover girl material, 'but I can see her getting work in fashion or in magazines like *The Face*.' Despite Lorraine's reservations, Jenny Richards gets a call-back, along with two other girls – Jenny Davies and Becky. This is the highest number of girls that the panel has picked from a single line-up

## BRISTOL – Day Two
### Marriott Hotel

**9.00am** Twenty model wannabes have turned up for the second day of auditioning and the panel now faces the difficult task of reducing the selection down further to only four girls. After watching them do a short walk up and down the red carpet, the judges retire to cogitate. 'It's one of the hardest decisions we've ever had to make,' admits Lorraine.

**10.30am** Ten girls have already been given their marching orders. The remainder must now use cleansing tissues to wipe away their war paint and reveal their true selves. Despite the fact that she works in make-up for a living, Layla actually uses very little herself; others in the group wear more. Jenny Richards says she looks terrible with loads of make-up on. Jenny Davies admits, 'It's a bit scary taking everything off in front of the cameras – no concealer, no eyeliner!'

**11.30am** Lorraine works her way up the line and tells the girls that she thinks they all look far better without make-up.

Angus, Ollie and Lorraine at work.

**12.30pm** It's time to change into the *Model Behaviour* uniform – a revealing black top and shorts. For some of the potential cover girls, this is not what they expected. 'It was shocking to be asked to wear the black two-piece, but if that's what they needed to see us in, then fine,' comments Maisie. The girls' embarrassment is plain to see as they walk down the catwalk, tugging down their shorts and pulling up their tops. Jenny R, on the other hand, had no problems wearing the outfit, 'It was good walking down the catwalk in the black two-piece,' she says. 'I enjoyed it.'

**2.30pm** Interviews with all ten remaining competitors begin and as each girl gets a grilling the others wait in anticipation, knowing this is their last chance to make an impression. When asked if she'll be disappointed if

This line-up in Bristol is to be one of the strongest the judges have seen, with Jenny D, Rebecca and Jenny R all through.

Alexandria and Jenny D remove their make-up.

she doesn't get through, Layla is philosophical: 'Though I would be disappointed, this isn't the be-all and end-all. There will be other opportunities.'

**3.00pm** Alexandria doesn't think she is at all beautiful and tells the judges that she has no idea why they have picked her. Meanwhile, sixteen-year-old Becky isn't happy at the prospect of having all her hair cut off – the judges feel it is 'too big'.

**4.30pm** The interviews are over and the judges now have to make some very tough decisions. The quality of the girls at Bristol has been amazing, as Lorraine confirms: 'Overall, they are all of a high standard.'

**5.00pm** The panel discusses each girl in turn, highlighting her good points and noting her bad ones: 'Maisie is a definite,' says Ollie; 'Her height goes against her,' argues Angus. 'Layla is one of my favourites,' says Ollie. 'Jenny is amazing, she has fantastic bone structure and a brilliant personality,' gushes Angus. 'I was against her initially, but she has really won me over,' admits Lorraine. Becky with the 'big hair' is proving popular too: 'She's very together,' says Lorraine. 'Brilliant smile, lovely personality – we'd be mad not to take her,' agrees Angus.

**5.45pm** Finally the waiting is over, and the die is cast. In an unprecedented move, the panel has decided to take five girls to London with them because of the exceptional standard of the seven remaining Bristol girls. They are... Jenny Davies, Jenny Richards, Layla, Maisie and Becky. All five will travel to London for workshop week – but which, if any, will end up in the Model Apartment...?

> **'All the girls from Bristol got really close and got to know each other really well. We had a good time at the auditions.'**
> *Maisie, Bristol*

# so, you wanna be a –
# model?

Do you look like a million dollars despite wearing yesterday's make-up and your dad's old shirt? Do your best mates reckon you make Gisele look rough? Is your mum always badgering you to enter modelling competitions? Maybe you want to be a model but don't know how to take the plunge – or even exactly what it is that models do.

If you want to give a career in modelling your best shot, then the first step is to learn what's involved. To help you get started, *Model Behaviour* gives you the inside track on the modelling industry – we explain the basics and the jargon and reveal how some of the world's most beautiful super-models got their first big break.

And... you have to know what you're letting yourself in for when you tread the path to becoming a model. For every supermodel

**'You immediately know if a girl with supermodel potential walks into your agency.'**
*Angus Munro, Head Booker – Premier Model Management*

that makes it to the top, there are thousands of girls who don't make it at all. Odds are that no matter how beautiful, how dedicated and how likeable you are, you probably won't succeed as a model. Let's face it, most of us have more chance of winning the Lottery than becoming the next Kate Moss. But you'll never know whether you have what it takes to be a catwalk queen unless you go for it...

## the model industry

There are many different areas of the modelling industry – some more desirable, and therefore harder to break into, than others – so it's worth exploring your options and deciding on the type of modelling work that would suit both your looks and your personality.

## catwalk modelling

Only the modelling elite is offered this type of work. Fashion modelling is not only the most glamorous type of modelling, it is often the highest paid. It's highly sought after and fashion designers can pick and choose who they use to model their collections. Models must be tall, slender and highly photogenic. They also have to have a particular look to meet the demands of the fashion designer and suit the collection.

Catwalk models are usually around 5' 9", but there are always exceptions to the rule – Kate Moss is only 5' 7", for instance

## commercial modelling

This category covers all modelling that is designed to promote a product. Products can be anything from face creams to breakfast cereal to designer label jeans. Product advertising has more flexible requirements than fashion advertising.

Commercial print modelling includes photographs taken to advertise products on billboards, in magazines and newspapers. It includes modelling for catalogues too and requirements are much more flexible than fashion modelling. Commercial modelling can be extremely lucrative and models that become the face for a campaign or brand are not only well paid but become household names too. Cindy Crawford was the face of Revlon, Elizabeth Hurley is identified with Estée Lauder, and Christy Turlington with Calvin Klein.

**'You have to accept you can either model or you can't. A lot of it is genetic and there's nothing you can do about that.'**
*Lorraine Candy,*
*Editor of* **Cosmopolitan**

TV advertising is another area of commercial modelling. It is also well paid and increases a model's exposure. Models can be anything from babies to old age pensioners – it depends on what the client's needs are. Hair products require models with healthy-looking hair, while toothpaste companies need someone with perfect white teeth.

## glamour modelling

Ironically, 'glamour' modelling is probably the least glamorous type. Glamour photographs generally have a sexual theme and models may have to reveal more of their bodies. It is illegal to use models under the age of eighteen without parental consent; this area can be more risky than more traditional fashion and commercial modelling (more on the dangers later!).

## body parts modelling

You may not have the height or figure for fashion or commercial modelling but that doesn't mean you'll never make it in the industry. If you have a perfect set of pins then you could be just what a client manufacturing stockings is looking for to promote their product. Body parts models specialize in one part of the body – hands, ears, neck, feet or bottom. Some agencies also specialize in petite or oversize models, so if you're small but perfectly formed it's worth checking these out.

Like most industries, modelling uses plenty of jargon, and unless you have a background in the business, you're gonna need some help understanding modelling terms. So, learn the lingo before taking the plunge... and follow our A–Z guide to becoming a model.

## AGENCY

An agency is a model's connection to the outside world. It is the pivot of her career. Clients call the agency to book a model. Bookers work on behalf of the model to manage her bookings, her calendar and collect her fees.

## AGENT (OR BOOKER)

Agents are like a model's best friend. They manage her career, they take care of her day-to-day needs when working and they negotiate her fees. Without an agent, a model wouldn't get any work and without models, an agent would have no work.

## BOOKOUT

When a model tells her agent she is unavailable to work due to professional or personal reasons.

## CASTINGS

A client calls a number of agencies and gets them to send a group of models to a meeting known as a casting. These are both exciting and extremely dull – exciting because this is the first step to get a modelling job, and dull because they involve standing around for ages. When your turn comes, you only get a few seconds to impress...

## CHART

Models have to know where they have to be, and what time they have to be there. So, they have a chart – a calendar of all their appointments – which is organized by the agency.

## CONFIRMATION

The word every model loves. When a model gets a confirmation it means a client likes what he or she sees and decides to use her for a job. The more of these you get the better.

## DAY RATE

What a model can earn for a day's work. This varies hugely from £400 to £10,000, depending on the job and the name. Supermodels can earn upwards of £25,000 a day.

## EDITORIAL MODELLING

Highest-paid, highest-profile work. Models doing this work appear in glossy fashion magazines such as *Vogue* and *Cosmopolitan*.

## FAME

The top twenty-five editorial models are known as supermodels and they have fame and fortune to go with their title. Supermodels are seen as big-name celebrities.

## GO-SEES

These are a little like castings but more selective. They increase a model's profile and allow her to sell herself on a more personal level. Models are specifically asked to go and see a client in a small group. This is their opportunity to make an impression without loads of other models hanging around and cramping their style.

## HAUTE COUTURE

French for 'High fashion'. Tailor-made clothes, which are very expensive.

## INSURANCE

Some models insure their bodies or faces. Christie Turlington insured her face for $1,000,000.

## JOB

At the end of the day, being a model is a job, just like any other. You work – you get paid.

## KILLING TIME

Models spend a huge amount of their time waiting. Waiting to be seen at auditions, waiting for a call, waiting to be made up...

## LOVE

Any model will tell you that being a cover girl and maintaining a relationship is hard work. Models spend a lot of time away and work unsociable hours.

## MOTHER AGENCY

The agency that discovers, develops and launches a new model.

## NAUGHTY

Turning up late for jobs, being rude to photographers and clients and partying too hard is a sure-fire way to get dropped. If you want to be a model, be good.

## OPTION

Being put on option means being put on hold for a job! A client may put a few models on option before selecting the one he wants for a job.

## PORTFOLIO

A model's book is her portfolio of pictures, which goes everywhere with her. It's a model's selling tool and what she shows to prospective clients.

## QUESTION

Ask questions. Young models are vulnerable to unscrupulous people acting as scouts or photographers, who are really more interested in their money. Always check someone's credentials if they offer you a photoshoot or signing and ask you for cash.

## RELAX

Always be yourself. Modelling isn't just about looking good; it's about feeling good too. Act natural and chill out.

## REQUEST

This is when a client calls your agent and specifically requests an appointment to meet you.

**'I think you've really got to want to be a model because it's a lot of hard work.'** *Jenny R*

## SCOUT

Anyone employed by an agency to look (scout) for new modelling talent. Scouts can work anywhere – shopping centres, bus stations, clubs or even at school.

## TEST SHOOTS

This is where an agency shoots a few photos of a new model to see what she looks like in print. Some girls look great in real life but it doesn't show through in photographs.

## UNDERAGE

If you're under sixteen, you can't sign up with an agency without the permission of a guardian. Beware anyone trying to hire you without seeking that permission.

## VERSACE

One of the top names in designer fashion along with Gaultier, Westwood, Chloe and Klein.

## X

Kiss and tell. Professional models shouldn't slag off other models or clients. The fashion industry is small and bad-mouthing your colleagues won't get you far.

## YOGA

Keeping fit and healthy is an essential part of being a good model. Stay trim in body and spirit by taking up yoga.

## ZED CARD

These cards are typically 5" x 7" and contain a selection of photos of a model and her vital statistics. Models leave these calling cards after meeting a client.

# changing faces

There is no such thing as the perfect look for a model. Each fashion designer, client or agency searches for a certain "look" and that "look" will change depending on the current trend, the type of job and the type of client. Over the last fifty years, the look of a model has changed dramatically with each new decade. So what's in today may not be the look of tomorrow.

## THE 1930s – FLAPPER FASHION

Before 1930, modelling was not seen as a career that a nice girl would enter into. The first magazines didn't feature models on their covers until the late thirties.

## THE 1940s – RATIONED RADIANCE

The wartime forties saw the introduction of above-the-knee hems, boxy jackets with padded shoulders and frugal fabrics and finishes. Christian Dior launched the New Look in 1949, heralding the beginning of a more prosperous look and longer hemlines for the next decade. But modelling was still not considered a serious career option.

## 1950s – GLAMOUR GIRLS

Models of this era were seen as goddesses – they had glamour, breeding and style. Big names of the period included Suzy Parker and Anne Gunning. The clothes were fitted, expensive and feminine.

## 1960s – MOD MODELLING

The Swingin' Sixties were a revolutionary period in the fashion industry. A new style of clothes paraded on the catwalk by designers like Biba and Mary Quant became available on the high street. Girls like Jean 'The Shrimp' Shrimpton and Twiggy were thin and were the first to become well-known personalities. Mini skirts, acid prints and kaftans were in.

## 1970s – UPTOWN GIRLS

In the seventies, anything went – from flares and platforms to punk and gothic. Models were healthy looking, glamorous and in demand. Big names such as Christie Brinkley, Jerry Hall and Cheryl Tiegs graced the pages and covers of magazines like *Vogue*. Models also began to earn serious money with the introduction of global advertising.

## 1980s – SUPERMODEL STYLE

Models made the transition to supermodels when they became known by their first name – Cindy, Naomi, Claudia and Christy. With celebrity status came fame and fortune, and fashion was seriously on the entertainment map. Style encompassed the idea of dressing for success – power suits, shoulder pads and the preppie look were in.

## 1990s – WAIF WEAR

Wasted chic makes its entrance. Waif-like models, such as Kate Moss, were very much in vogue. Clothes were a mixture of retro, grunge and hip-hop styles.

## 2000 – SUPERBODIES RULE

The backlash against the stick-thin, sallow-skinned look led to the arrival of ultra-sexy, athletic look of models such as Gisele Bundchen, Carmen Kass and Elle 'The Body' MacPherson. Clothes were sexy, svelte and always glamorous.

## 2001 – ANDROGYNOUS ART

The beginning of the twenty-first century is the year of the Belgian, with new talent such as Kim Peers, Roos van Bosstraeten and An Oost emerging. The look is bold, broody and defiant. Clothes are tailored and black is the new black.

On the catwalk this autumn/winter is an eclectic range of looks, including: the hour-glass figure with curvaceous waistlines and corsetry; the Victorian prim and pretty period style with high necklines and lace-up boots; sexy baby-doll glamour with flouncy frills and sheer fabrics; and pop-art patterns in bold, eye-catching colour and mismatched belts and bags.

If you've set your heart on being a model then don't let us stop you – it's great to have a goal in life. But, before you set out to follow your dream, make sure you are prepared. Prepared for the hard slog ahead. Prepared to be scrutinized and criticized. Prepared for hours of waiting around. And ultimately, you must be prepared for rejection.

If you still think you have what it takes to succeed in the modelling world, then the next step is to get signed with an agency. Read on for *Model Behaviour*'s step-by-step guide to getting started.

## *what it takes to be a model*
# top ten

❋ **1. LOOKS** Beauty is an essential requirement. Classical beauty is not always 'the look' that's in, though. 'The look' can change with the season, so don't despair if you're not a typical English Rose.

❋ **2. DETERMINATION** Modelling requires hard work and the schedules are tough. You must be prepared to work long hours at any time of the day or night.

❋ **3. FIGURE** Fashion models are usually, but not always, over 5' 7", with a figure that's in proportion.

❋ **4. INTELLIGENCE** You need to use your brain. There's a lot to learn in this business and you don't get much time to do it. It's important to appear professional and business-like when dealing with agents, clients and photographers.

❋ **5. STAMINA** Do you think you're hard enough? Long hours on your feet in stressful conditions aren't everybody's idea of fun. Make sure you can cope.

❋ **6. AMBITION** You have to have a goal. You won't be a successful cover girl if you sit about waiting for agents to come to you. If you want it badly enough, go get it.

❋ **7. ORGANIZATION** Models must manage their schedules efficiently. It's important they know where they should be and when, and always turn up on time.

❋ **8. PERSONALITY** There is more to modelling than a pretty face. Models must be person-able, lively and sociable.

❋ **9. CONFIDENCE** Clients look for someone who is self-assured and comfortable with being in the limelight. Shrinking violets need not apply.

❋ **10. SELF-BELIEF** Dealing with knock-backs is part and parcel of being a model. No model can meet the expectation of every client, so she has to be prepared for rejection without losing her self-esteem.

# workshop *week*

Only a tiny percentage of the 4,500 girls from up and down the land who took part in the regional auditions have made it to London to the *Model Behaviour* workshop week. Twenty-one excited young women turn up, eager to see what the next seven days have in store for them. Many have brought a member of their family or their partner to give moral support, as the week ahead is not going to be easy. Will they be one of the successful five who will spend the next few months living a model's life in London, or will they be going straight back home with nothing but memories to show for their trouble?

Catwalk coach Jay Alexander.

## Day One
### Monday 11 June 2001

Twenty-one potential supermodels arrive at the very swanky Hilton International in London. Not everyone's journey has been uneventful, though. Becks drove in and had a puncture on the way, fixing it with Sellotape. After checking in and quickly unpacking their gear, the girls rush down into the lobby, where they'll be meeting up with the TV crew. From here it's off to a dance studio in west London, where the selection process really begins.

The first person they meet is the fashion industry's catwalk king, Jay Alexander, a fashion show producer who has taught the likes of Naomi Campbell and Elle MacPherson how to work the runway. Jay will be assessing the girls' catwalk skills — and he doesn't take any prisoners. 'Jay Alexander is an immensely tall bloke, and he wore a pair of high heels. He would make some evil comments, but luckily I escaped,' recalls Chermaine.

Jay tells the girls some important things to remember: 'You are ladies — pamper yourselves. No nasty toenails or fingernails. The most important thing? No little hairy monsters where there shouldn't be any.' He asks the girls if anyone has ever had catwalk experience before (only Samantha has), and then settles down to the task of showing the girls how to walk. 'That was so funny. It was a bit scary to start with but it was

Jenny R applies a final touch of lip gloss.

Jay Alexander shows the girls how to work the catwalk.

good,' reveals Jenny Richards. 'I thought Jay Alexander was great, he was fantastic… absolutely amazing and a really good character,' says Alicia.

As each girl walks the catwalk, Jay comments on their poise, body language and confidence. Samantha comes under fire for her walk, which Jay says is too loose, and Nyathesis is asked to relax her face. 'You look mad!' Jay exclaims and sets off down the catwalk saying, 'Look like this, so you're thinking, "I know I look stupid, but it's okay."' Other girls are accused of walking too fast, or of looking down at their feet. Jay explains that walking the runway is all about you. He wants the girls to do it right and tells them, 'It's good to look at yourself in the mirror so you can make corrections.'

After a day of walking in front of all the other wannabe models and the ruthlessly critical Jay, the girls are all nervous about what tomorrow holds in store for them, as Angus reveals that only half will be staying after Tuesday. The girls go back to the hotel for dinner, but the tension is obvious as the nerves start to show. Sophie admits that, 'If they kick me out tomorrow I'll be very upset.' Samantha is worried about her decision to pass on the model audition she had lined up in Brazil to

come to the *Model Behaviour* workshop week, 'If it all goes wrong I'll think I should have gone to Brazil,' she frets. Lara is adamant that she really doesn't want to go home. 'I totally don't want to go,' she says. 'I think I'm going home tomorrow, but I don't want to.'

## Day Two
### Tuesday 12 June 2001

Eleven of the twenty-one finalists will be going home this lunchtime and the girls are understandably very anxious. Having got this far, none of them wants to be rejected just yet. 'I've been terrible all morning,' wails Layla, 'I've been walking so fast, so now I am going to walk really slowly on the catwalk and not let Jay intimidate me.' It's a wise decision, because the catwalk is a crucial part of the decision-making process. This morning the girls will have to walk with Jay, watched by the judges – Ollie, Lorraine and Angus – who will assess them on their walk, confidence, poise and on how comfortable they look on the catwalk.

To make matters worse, it's not only high heels that they will have to contend with. Walking with

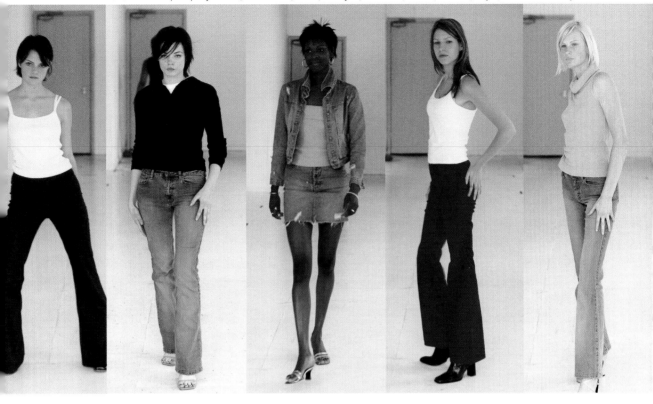

The ten finalists (l to r): Nyathesis, Chermaine, Alicia, Jenny D, Elizabeth, Maisie, Patricia, Layla, Becks and Jenny R.

scarves and low hemlines are just two of the hazards the girls will have to master to be successful runway models. 'The first day we did catwalk practising, Jay watched us, and the second day we had to wear different costumes and walk in front of the judges. Jay would wear a long, flowing dress or ball gown and then we would have to copy him,' remembers Chermaine. If they don't make the grade on the catwalk, the girls' dreams of becoming a professional model will be shattered.

Each girl then takes a deep breath and begins the hardest walk of the selection process so far. After all twenty-one have shown their runway skills, they sit in a group while the judges make their decision about who is going and who is staying... It's crunch time, and the girls are crawling the walls in anticipation. 'I think everyone is really worried now,' says Jenny Davies. Even madcap Becks is thoughtful: 'I think at every stage that's gone I have got less positive as it gets more serious. I think they'll think, "Right, it's time to let the nutter go now."' Jenny Richards is confident she will be going home too. 'I am really nervous because I don't think I'll be getting through,' she sighs.

Alicia just wants the suspense to end: 'I'm only doing this to earn some cash for some nice shoes,' she jokes. Despite being just seventeen years old, Maisie has a much calmer outlook on the whole event than some of her elders: 'I have a view on life – don't expect anything. Then when it happens, you'll be glad. If it doesn't, you won't be disappointed.'

After much deliberation and discussion, the judges think they are close to a final selection. It's been a tough process. 'This is probably the most difficult part – going to just ten – so we do need to be unnecessarily harsh,' notes Lorraine. One hour later, the panel emerges to give the girls its final verdict.

Angus gets straight to the point, after thanking the girls for taking part: 'If I call out your name, city and number, you will be staying.' The tension is unbearable as the girls are called to the front one by one... First up is Nyathesis, followed by Elizabeth, Alicia, Jenny Richards, Chermaine, Maisie, Patricia, Layla, Becks and Jenny Davies. The girls whoop with delight and hug, while the other eleven look on, wishing they were staying on for the rest of the week.

Elizabeth feels that she had an instinct she'd get

Waiting around...

... Maisie, Patricia and Chermaine chill out.

Becks has her make-up done by Mark Cook.

through, even though the catwalk wasn't her strongest area: 'They put us in a big room and said "If we call your name out you are staying on." Angus came in and I remember he smiled at me and that really boosted my confidence, because I didn't think he would have smiled at me if I wasn't through.' Alicia had mixed feelings about her selection: 'After the second day I had really had enough and I was disappointed not to be going back home.' Patricia, despite being through, found the other girls' anguish very upsetting: 'I got more and more shocked when I got through each of the stages. I couldn't understand why I was being chosen. I was really pleased, but it wasn't nice seeing other girls crying.'

Having announced the gonnabes, Angus then tells the wannabes that they've all been brilliant, in an attempt to make them feel better about themselves. But some are inconsolable, including Samantha, who passed up the chance of entering the Elite Model Competition in Brazil to come to the workshop week in London. 'I had a ticket waiting and now I have nothing, so I am *not* all right,' she says, sobbing. Rebecca too is in tears, and Sophie complains that sitting waiting for an hour was the most awful experience so far. The judges didn't escape the effects of the pressure, either. 'It wasn't easy to turn girls away,' reveals Angus. 'It was high stress with cameras around. It was quite a cruel selection process in a way, because they had no idea and there was a lot of waiting around. Normally a girl would walk into Premier and I'd say, "You may have it but you're not right for here." It was a long drawn-out, protracted process and I think that was hard for them.'

With the losers all returning home, Ollie then congratulates the winners and tells them what's in store over the next few days: 'We are going to be involving you in different processes all week up until Saturday, when we will choose five of you to come to move into the Model Apartment. The winners will live together for three months and get the chance to be a professional model.' He goes on to prepare the girls for the fact that the next phase is likely to be the most difficult, because by the end of the week they will have bonded. To relieve the tension, Angus asks the girls to give themselves a big cheer and a clap, something they do with gusto... it pays to have confidence at times like this.

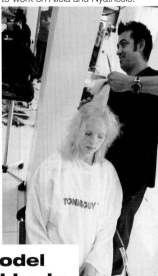

Anthony Mascolo and his team get to work on Alicia and Nyathesis.

> **'To be a good model you have a good body, bone shape, to be patient, be happy and get on with people well.'** *Elizabeth*

## Day Three
### Wednesday 13 June 2001

With the pressure and excitement of the last two days behind them, the ten finalists look forward to the highlight of the whole selection process so far – a complete makeover. Each girl has a personal consultation with a team of fashion experts that includes Anthony Mascolo, Art Director of Toni & Guy, fashion stylist Charty Durrant, fashion photographer Donna Francesca and make-up artist Mark Cook. The professionals discuss each girl's current look with the judges and come up with a new image to launch her on a potential career as a cover girl. 'We met the girls and discussed the image we were going to give them. That was done at the T&G salon and the girls were scrutinized and filmed. There were a few arguments,' reveals Donna. 'It was quite a transformation,' agrees Charty.

First, the judges look at Jenny Davies, and Ollie persuades her to have her long hair cut a little shorter. Anthony wants to remove Layla's hair extensions, and she agrees,

while Angus says that Chermaine is one girl who could really carry a 'mad haircut'. With the rough styles decided, it's off to the Toni & Guy salon for Anthony's team of stylists to do the business on the girls' tresses. Alicia isn't happy about all this attention: 'I hate having my hair touched.' Most of the girls have a change of style, but it's Maisie and Chermaine who have the most dramatic cuts. 'It's really short,' comments Maisie, 'but I like it.' Chermaine certainly does get a mad haircut, but it's not to everyone's taste – including hers: 'I didn't get any say on how my hair was cut. I am growing it out now. It was a called a Mullet, apparently.' 'I didn't like Chermaine's haircut – they made it look quite sixties,' observes Donna.

The make-up artist, Mark, was then given a loose brief to make the girls look as gorgeous as he could: 'I tried to do a natural look that enhanced the girls' own beauty.' Mark talks about the extent to which make-up can transform a woman's appearance: 'So many girls come in to be made up whom you wouldn't look twice at, but when they've had their hair and make-up done they look amazing.' Ollie agrees: 'You see a beautiful girl walking down the road and you think, "God, she must be a model", you take a picture of her and she looks awful. It can work the other way round too. A girl can walk into my hairdressing salon and I think, "God, she can't be a model." You do her up and put her in the clothes and take a picture of her and you can't believe it's the same girl.'

All of the girls were pleased with their new looks, including Maisie. 'They wanted to keep me natural because I've got a natural look,' she confides. Jenny Davies has beautiful porcelain skin, which looks dramatic against her dark shaggy hair, and the natural make-up that Mark gives her enhances the effect. Patricia gets a glam look with glossy red lips, and Elizabeth has been given a sultry look with smudged dark liner and shadow. Jenny Richards has a very fair, translucent complexion and Mark uses only the minimum of make-up to warm up her face and define her eyes.

After the make-up and the hair, it's time to choose the clothes. Stylist Charty Durrant explains what her role is: 'I prepare for the photoshoot. The idea was to work on doing an individual look for each girl because they were all so individual looking. I wanted to do something that would work both for a fashion show and in photographs.' Charty, who has worked with loads of celebrities, including Geri Halliwell and Mel B,

had £15,000 worth of designer clothes and shoes for the girls to wear – and all were keen to do so! 'I chose a selection of clothes for each girl to choose from,' Charty explains. 'I tried to dress them to suit their characters as well as their physical form.'

After much dressing and undressing, the ten finally have an outfit to wear for the photoshoot taking place the next day. And they can't wait to show off their new images.

## Day Four
### Thursday 14 June 2001

It's nearly the end of the week, and the girls are about to have their photograph taken by top fashion photographer Donna Francesca. Unusually, she'll be taking extra-large Polaroids of the girls so the judges can use these to aid them in their decision to choose the lucky five who will be moving into the *Model Behaviour* apartment. To be a *Cosmo* cover girl, it's important to have a face that photographs well, as Lorraine explains: 'Her face has to be fairly symmetrical. She has to be able to smile with her eyes and look warm. There are so few models that can do that.'

Alicia comes to the attention of photographer Donna: 'Once she was in front of the camera, she just worked. She was almost kissing that lens because she was really confident in herself and happy in front of the camera.' Not everyone was so at ease, however. Layla found it very difficult to pose in front of the camera. Each girl had her own particular talent and each fashion professional had their own opinions on the finalists, as they reveal. 'Elizabeth looked fabulous, though her look isn't necessarily my cup of tea,' says Donna. 'Jenny has gorgeous long legs. Very blonde and quite androgynous looking – a bit punky.'

'I think Patricia is fantastic, She's got an amazing face. She photographs well. If her skin was perfect I think she would model,' says Lorraine, while Donna observes that, 'Patricia has a modern Audrey Hepburn look about her.'

Angus, though pleased with the girls selected, admits that none were exactly what he was hoping

Elizabeth, Layla and Alicia waiting for their turn in the spotlight.

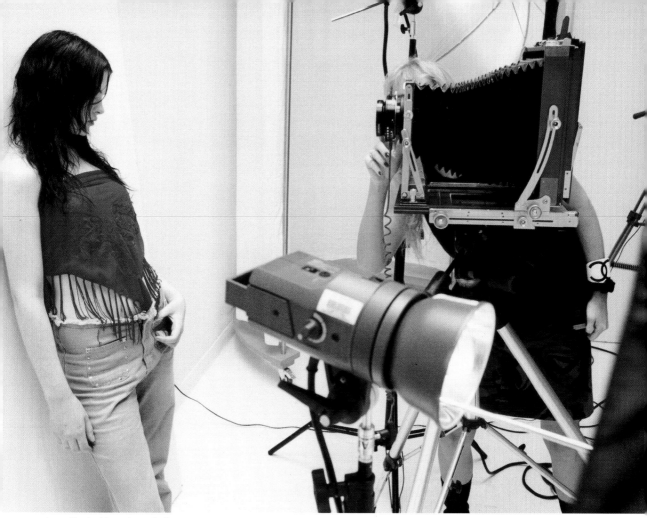

Jenny Davies' brand new look.

It's been a long day...

for. 'All of the girls have some potential in one way or the other.' But the girls themselves were delighted with the end results, 'When I saw the photo of myself I couldn't believe it was me,' enthuses Maisie.

## Day Five
### Friday 15 June 2001

All ten girls have had a fabulous week, and no one wants to go home. Sadly, only half will be told they are going through to the final stage – to live in the *Model Behaviour* apartment in the heart of the capital. Having spent a week together, many of the girls have become quite close, so they're as anxious for their friends as they are for themselves. 'I just want to do the show,' says Layla. 'It's what we've been waiting for all week.'

The panel has arrived to watch the girls perform on the catwalk for the last time. Also watching are the girls' families and friends, as well as experts from the fashion

**'I'm a teenager and teenagers are supposed to get spots.'**
*Patricia*

industry. How well they do here will mean the difference between success and failure; nerves are frayed and the tension is mounting. So, what do the girls think about the impending decision? 'Either way, I'll be excited and relieved. I'm looking forward to going home now,' reveals Nyathesis, 'and I really want to get on with the show.' Elizabeth reckons the panel thinks she isn't confident because she is so quiet, but she knows otherwise: 'I'm not shy, I just like to get to know people before I get loud.' Jenny Davies thinks the judges have a good idea of who they're going to pick before the show, 'They've spent a week with us so they must have an idea already. I think the show is just a formality.'

It's crunch time as the music starts and the girls line up backstage, waiting for their turn to walk the runway. This, more than any other moment so far, is the crucial test, and now the girls have a final chance to show the panel that they have the potential to go all the way as a model. Patricia hates the runway: 'Having to learn to walk on the catwalk was probably the most

Last-minute advice before the final catwalk show.

PLEASE! DO NOT WALK SO FAST TAKE YOUR TIME...

BE PROUD YOU ARE A STAR AT LEAST FOR NOW?

NO! NAME CALLING.... 4 OR 5 LETTER WORDS NOT ACCEPTED...

PLEASE! NO HUNCH BACKS!

FOR ALL THINK! WINNER....

NO! CRAB CLAWS ON HIPS.....

nerve-racking thing ever. I really hated it, though I think I'm the only one who doesn't like the catwalk.' Maisie, however, enjoyed the experience: 'The catwalk was amazing, really. Everything we did that week was a whole new experience for me.'

First to walk is Jenny Davies... last on the catwalk is Layla, who returns to the other girls waiting backstage. She is so relieved to have completed the walk that she burst into tears — much to the horror of the others, who cry, 'Your make-up, your make-up!' and tell her to pull herself together, because they're about to walk out and line up together for the last time...

## Day Six
### Saturday 16 June 2001

The final decision on who will go through to have the chance of becoming a professional model rests with the judges. With the help of the two Polaroids taken by Donna, and catwalk film footage, the judges will scrutinize each girl in turn until they can decide which five they must eliminate. It's not going to be easy...

'In selecting the five from ten our task was very difficult,' confirms Ollie. When you get to know them it's harder, as you want to be impartial and really you don't want to choose any of them, in a way. We had to see them in print at this point and that was amazing,' he admits. 'Once we'd seen them in print we got a much better idea of whether they'd work as models.'

Being a model is all about confidence, personality and poise, as Maisie demonstrates.

But the judges also had to take into account other factors, such as each girl's catwalk ability, her personality and whether she has the right temperament for life as a model... 'Of the ten, looking at them, I knew that three of them would be probably be selected for the final five. But it was important for the TV production company to have the right mix of girls to live in the house as well,' explains Angus. The judges were also looking for different qualities, as Ollie divulges: 'I was looking for someone with a quirky sort of face. I personally wasn't looking for someone like Claudia Schiffer, with the supermodel type of face that was left in the eighties. I don't think you'll find someone like Gisele in England – that Brazilian look – so it was more quirky people like Kate Moss, who is also beautiful.'

'I want someone who can make eye-contact on the news-stands when people are scanning the magazines. Someone that looks approachable, inspirational and glamorous. A very commercial girl who is sexy, healthy and glows, whose personality shines through,' says Lorraine. Angus has his own criteria too: 'The kind of models I like are very striking. I like striking girls who can do both types of work – fashion editorial and commercial modelling. Business-wise, that's the best too.'

While the judges cogitate and deliberate, the ten finalists are taken to a swanky London restaurant for a meal, where they'll be left waiting for two hours before they hear their fate. It's their Last Supper, because at the end of it, Lorraine, Angus and Ollie will be revealing the names of the girls who have been selected to move to London, and the ones that will be heading back home empty handed.

The time has come to reveal the five finalists and as the panel joins the ten beautiful model wannabes, there is frisson of anticipation and excitement. The girls have their family or friends with them for support, and the judges begin their announcements. Angus begins by congratulating the group and telling them, 'You should all be proud of your-

The girls take a trip on the London Eye.

Patrica and Maisie give each other much needed support.

West

selves.' Each girl is then told their fate one by one, in front of the rest of the hopefuls. The atmosphere is unbearably tense as the first name is called...

'Patricia,' Angus announces, 'when we first saw you we all picked you out straight away. There was the skin thing that we were concerned about. That is a tricky thing to get around... Congratulations, you are going to be a professional model.' Patricia grins from ear to ear and is hugged by her friend. 'I wasn't that nervous about finding out if I was in the final five,' she confesses. 'I just wanted to get told. I was thinking, "If I don't get through, I don't get through and I can go home." I wanted to get though but I wouldn't have cried or anything if I didn't.'

## 'Do not take it too seriously. It's a great way to earn lots of money and have a laugh.'
### Charty Durrant, stylist

Next is Jenny Davies. 'Yours was a very difficult decision. You have amazing skin and a beautiful face. We were concerned about your height, though,' Lorraine says. Angus takes over: 'It's a good face for beauty, but fashion is a different thing. You won't be joining us in the apartment.' Jenny is obviously distressed and fights back the tears. Becks dabs a tear from her eye as she watches Jenny in distress. 'Be horrible to me,' Jenny tells everyone, 'if you're nice, I'll cry.' Lorraine then tells

Jenny Richards is distraught to hear it's the end of the road for her.

Becks and Layla congratulate Maisie on getting through.

Nyathesis the bad news: 'You have a distinct look. It was difficult for us to decide, as you have a singularly individual look, but we have decided...' 'Sorry, Thesis, you won't be joining us for the final,' Angus finishes. Nyathesis remains positive, despite her disappointment. It's then Maisie's turn, and Angus delivers the verdict on her: 'You take a fantastic picture and the haircut has really made a difference to your face. You will be joining us.' Maisie is obviously delighted and shocked at the news, and her mother gives her a congratulatory hug.

Next is Layla, and she looks terrified about what she may be told... 'You've been a diamond,' says Ollie. 'But,' continues Angus, 'I was concerned that, though you are striking, you don't take a good picture and the light isn't kind to your face. You will not be joining us.' Layla looks downcast, but insists she's okay. Becks gives her a consoling hug. It's then Alicia's turn, and Angus doesn't pull any punches. 'Alicia, when we picked you in Manchester we thought you didn't want to do it.' Lorraine has her say too: 'You had some kind of attitude.' 'We thought you didn't want to be there and that other people would want it far more... But then we decided to congratulate you and ask you to join us,' Angus finishes. Alicia, who has sat stony faced throughout, visibly relaxes and grins like the Cheshire Cat. Boyfriend Barry is made up too: 'That's my girl!' he says.

So far, three girls have made it to the final and three have been rejected. There are now only two places left, and four girls await their future with anxiety. Elizabeth is soon put out of her misery, as Angus begins, 'We were

unsure about you because you're really quiet.' 'You're obviously bright and intelligent,' observes Angus, 'and I think you walk abysmally, but your pictures were great, among the best, so we'd like to congratulate you.' Elizabeth looks reservedly happy as usual, until pushed by the others to show her feelings and screaming with excitement. 'If I hadn't got through I would have been quite relaxed, because I would have had my summer holidays,' she says.

Next is Jenny and she looks pale and worried as Angus tells her the panel's final decision, 'You were the most difficult decision. You have a very individual look and in modelling terms you have the best profile I have ever seen... We have decided that you will not be coming with us.' Jenny is devastated and can't hold back the torrent of tears. She wipes at her eyes, smudging her mascara; the girls around her can't stand to see her distress, and burst into tears themselves...

With only two girls left now, and one place available, Angus decides to address them both together, 'One of you will get through, one will not.' 'Both of you are amazing people,' chips in Ollie. 'Chermaine has a very distinctive face, which will be good for editorial. Becks has a strong face that is unusual in fashion. We had to look at who was more comfortable behind the camera and so, Chermaine, you are through. Sorry, Becks, you will not be joining us.' Chermaine is surprised at the decision, while Becks is beside herself, as Chermaine recalls: 'That was one of the worst moments. It was between me and Becky, so we had to be told together. It was difficult, because we'd gone through the competition together until then. The judges told us I had got through and she went really mental, and I was shocked and really sad because she was upset and blamed me.'

Many of the final five were sad their fellow competitors hadn't been as lucky as they had. 'I felt very bad for Thesis when she didn't get in, but she congratulated me and really meant it. That meant a lot to me,' remembers Alicia. Elizabeth recalls feeling confused: 'Some people didn't want to get through; some people really wanted to get through. I kept changing my mind and about two seconds before I was told, I really wanted to get through.'

Jenny Richards was probably the most affected of all the girls: 'It was really, really horrible and I was really upset,' she sighs. 'The people who got through, the judges were really negative with; but with me, it was, "You're really, really pretty, the judges loved you but you haven't got through." I was gutted.' 'Jenny was probably the most upset when she didn't get through. I just cried watching them cry. It was really emotional,' admits Patricia. 'I felt for Thesis, and Layla, because she really wanted to get through. I was quite upset for Jenny too because she really wanted it,' reveals Elizabeth. 'I got upset when five were rejected, because

it was so emotional. The five who got through couldn't be happy because the others hadn't,' Maisie sighs.

The judges found the whole selection process draining and emotional too, and were glad when it was all over. 'The worst part was letting five of the ten go. The five who were dismissed didn't get the chance to go anywhere and you are a loser if you are one of those final five not selected,' acknowledges Angus. Lorraine reveals that for all their hard-hearted appearance, the panellists found the whole experience of rejecting people at this late stage very difficult to do: 'All the girls were lovely and it was horrible to see them go. I felt mean, it was like treading on a small puppy – it was a rotten thing to have to do'. 'Choosing the final five from the ten was probably the worst bit for me,' confesses Ollie. 'It was the hardest thing to decide who to pick. I don't even know if we made the right decisions. You had to go with your instinct at that time. When you're on camera having to make those decisions, it's even harder.'

With workshop week over, five girls go home feeling rejected but pleased that they had made it this far and experienced so much. For the winners, there is only a week to get themselves sorted out to be ready to move into the *Model Behaviour* Apartment – this is just the beginning...

Dreams are shattered and ambitions realised as the results are announced.

# have you got what it takes?

You've taken the first step and decided to be a cover girl, so now it's time to find out whether you have the potential to succeed in the competitive world of modelling.

For a start, you'll need to be tall. No matter how much your desire to be a model, if you're 4' 5" it's not gonna happen. There's a chance you could get work modelling petite clothes ranges for catalogues or shops, but only a slim one. If you have bad teeth, bad hair or a skin problem, you'll have to work that bit harder, but you can do it! If you hate being the centre of attention, though, perhaps you should think again – not everyone can be suited to a particular career. You might want to be a Spitfire pilot but don't have the skills or temperament to succeed; that doesn't mean you're a failure. It's the same for modelling.

So, with that thought in mind, why not have some fun entering the *Model Behaviour* quiz to discover...

## HAVE YOU *REALLY* GOT WHAT IT TAKES TO BE A MODEL?

✳ **1. When you buy clothes you head for the nearest:**
- ☑ a.  High-street store selling size 6–10
- ☐ b.  Next kids' range
- ☐ c.  Oversize rack

✳ **2. You want to go out on the town with your mates but you are grounded. Do you?**
- ☐ a.  Accept that you deserved to be grounded, and look forward to going out next week instead
- ☑ b.  Plead with your mum and offer to do the dishes for a week in the hope she agrees
- ☐ c.  Shout and scream and stamp your feet, and then slip out of your bedroom window leaving a pillow in your bed

3. You have been asked to take a role in your college play and you instantly agree. When you find out that you are not in the starring role but only in support you are:

- [✓] a. Pleased to have been selected at all. You throw yourself into the role in the hope that you'll get noticed for the leading part next time
- [ ] b. Disappointed, so you reluctantly go to rehearsals and sulk in the wings
- [ ] c. Furious and refuse to take part

4. How would you best describe your relationship with your parents?

- [✓] a. Fantastic. You love shopping with your mum and spending time with the family as well as going out with your friends
- [ ] b. Embarrassing. Your parents don't understand you and you don't understand them. You spend as much time out of the house as possible
- [ ] c. Horrendous. You can't stand to be in the same room as them and rebel at every opportunity

5. You've been out on the town and you get back late. Do you:

- [✓] a. Remove all your make-up, and tone and moisturize before crawling into your pit
- [ ] b. Clean your teeth, remove your party clothes and then collapse under the duvet
- [ ] c. Flop straight to bed complete with all your clothes and make-up

6. A handsome older guy insists on buying you an alcoholic drink, but you're under age. Do you:

- [ ] a. Say no thank you very much and head home
- [✓] b. Accept, but tip it into a handy pot plant when no one's looking
- [ ] c. Order a double – being drunk sounds like great fun

7. A new girl has just joined your dance class. You want to make friends, but your best pal hates her and asks you to ignore her. Do you:

- [✓] a. Tell your friend that as much as you like her you are not going to be nasty to someone else for her
- [ ] b. Go off with the new girl and dump your friend
- [ ] c. Do as she asks and bitch about the new girl to all your other mates

8. You're starving hungry and need a snack. Which of these foods would you automatically go for?

- [ ] a. A healthy bowl of fresh fruit
- [ ] b. A bacon sandwich on wholemeal bread with plenty of ketchup
- [✓] c. A giant-sized Mars bar

9. It's the night before you go on holiday and you have to be up at 4.00 a.m. for the flight. Are you planning to?

- [✓] a. Finish off packing and go to bed early
- [ ] b. Go out with your mate, 'cos you won't see her for two weeks, leaving a pile of clothes and an empty case
- [ ] c. Go down to the laundrette to wash and dry the clothes you want to take with you

✤ 10. You've seen a fab new jacket that you're dying to buy. It's a hundred quid and you have only fifty. How do you get the rest of the cash?
- [ ] a. Take on a few extra errands and earn the money yourself
- [ ] b. Borrow the money from your little sister's piggy bank
- [✓] c. Whinge and whine at your parents until they give you the dosh

✤ 11. You are going to the dentist. Do you:
- [✓] a. Get there five minutes before the appointment, calm and collected
- [ ] b. Rush in the door with your breakfast in your hand
- [ ] c. Wander in ten minutes late without a care in the world

✤ 12. The clothes you took off last night are now:
- [ ] a. Hung neatly in your wardrobe, or in the washbasket
- [✗] b. Carelessly tossed on your bed or down beside the washbasket
- [ ] c. Hung on your floor in a crumpled heap along with yesterday's cereal bowl and a half-eaten banana

✤ 13. You have an important assignment that you were given two weeks ago. The night before it's due you are:
- [✗] a. Having a last read through to make sure you've got everything correct
- [ ] b. Watching telly 'cos you finished it yesterday
- [ ] c. Frantically telephoning all your mates to see if you can copy theirs

✤ 14. Your favourite magazine is:
- [✗] a. *Cosmo* or *Vogue*
- [ ] b. *Smash Hits* or *TOTP*
- [ ] c. The Teletubbies magazine 'cos you love La La

✤ 15. When you go shopping, people ask you:
- [✓] a. To kindly reach that packet of cereal on the top shelf for them
- [ ] b. Whether you would like some help getting down a packet of crisps
- [ ] c. Whether you should be out on your own without your mum

For all A answers score 3, for Bs score 2 and for Cs score 1. Add them all up to work out whether you are likely to become the next Cindy Crawford.

If you scored above 35 points you should be feeling pleased. You are on the right track to a career in modelling and have the basic ingredients needed to be a cover girl of the future.

If you scored between 19–34, you may have the potential to be a model but there's a lot you need to improve first. Check back to see where you scored badly, and work on improving those areas.

If you scored 18 or under you might want to consider changing your intended career path. You are probably a great laugh, but let's face it you don't want to grow up just yet – you just want to have a ball.

If you reckon you have the right qualities then the first thing you have to do is find out whether a professional modelling agency agrees with you. Though there are a few ways to enter the business, the one most wannabe models take is to find an agency.

## finding an agency

Do some research before you start looking for an agency. The biggest are usually in major cities, where you also find fashion designers and fashion photographers. London is the obvious place, though agencies can be found in cities such as Manchester and Birmingham too. Provincial towns also have agencies, but these are usually much smaller, so if you are determined to be a model you will have to accept that you will ultimately have to move to the capital if you are successful.

Make sure you choose well-known, reputable agencies to contact. There are many disreputable outfits willing to tell you that you are beautiful so they can take your money. Good professional agencies won't ask you for any money up front – they train you free.

Most big agencies have a specific time allocated to open auditions, where aspiring models can drop in. Premier offers open call between 10.00am and noon from Monday to Friday. It is worth checking beforehand what you should bring with you. At the very least, they will expect to see a couple of decent close-up pictures, as well as your personal details, such as body measurements, weight and dress size. The more prepared you are, the more professional and serious about a career in modelling you'll look.

Listen to the agency staff's advice – they will tell you if they think you have the potential to be a model.

> **'Certain people have that _je ne sais quoi_ – the way they dress, the way they carry themselves – that's what makes them beautiful.'**
> _Oliver Woods, Judge_

## what does the agency do?

1. They find new talent
2. They advise and train their models
3. They promote models and manage their careers
4. They schedule and book the models
5. They bill clients and negotiate their models' fees

> **'If you are a sensitive person and care about what people say about you, then don't go into modelling.'**
> _Patricia_

## signing with an agency

Don't sign with the first agency you visit. Go and see at least three before you decide which one to join, assuming you've been lucky enough to have been offered a contract. If you have seen over a dozen agencies and not been offered a signing then, sorry, you have to face the fact that you may not succeed in the fashion modelling business. Perhaps you could try a different area of modelling, like body parts, or choose a different career altogether. There are other areas within the fashion industry in which you can forge a career.

Before signing a contract, get a parent or friend to go through it in detail with you. If you are not sure about any of the terms ask the agency what they mean. And remember, *always* read the small print.

# avoiding modelling scams

The fashion modelling industry is a cutthroat one, and there are plenty of con artists out there who will promise you the world in return for your cash. Beware modelling scams like being asked to sign a contract at a photoshoot. Unprofessional photographers may want you to sign over the rights to the photographs so you have no control how they are used. Even experienced models can be scammed – supermodel Laetitia Casta discovered her picture was being used to promote an escort ad in a magazine. We've produced a checklist of the major scams to look out for:

**'Be careful and always ask others for advice before you go into modelling.'**
*Elizabeth*

### MISLEADING MODELLING SCHOOLS

Dodgy modelling schools that offer guaranteed work, limited places and the chance to produce a "complete portfolio" using their own photographers should be avoided. If you feel you really want to go to a school (it isn't absolutely necessary), then do your homework first. Ask the obvious questions. Have any of the school's graduates gone on to be successful? Does the school display their model's tear sheets? Are they registered? Do scouts from major agencies visit?

Just because you attended a modelling school, it doesn't automatically mean you can model, so bear this in mind.

### SHADY SNAPPERS

If a school or photographer offers a complete portfolio of pictures, leave well alone. A good portfolio is built over time, and includes tear sheets of a model's work, as well as a selection of good-quality pictures. A decent agency won't expect you to audition with a complete portfolio – a couple of snapshots will do. Spending a fortune on getting a load of pictures is a complete waste of money, time and effort. If you do decide to get a set of professional photographs, ask to see the photographer's work, get a fixed price for the photos and make sure you take someone along with you for the shoot.

### ARTFUL AGENCIES

An agency should realistically assess your chances of becoming a model. They should not push you into signing a contract, and they should always ask to contact your parents or guardian if you are under eighteen.

**'Eat well. Eat healthy. Don't worry about your weight and being pencil thin.'**
*Rafah Sabbagh, Chaperone*

Reputable agencies will not ask you for a fee up front for training or to produce your first set of test shots. They should also be happy to give you any information you want about their clients and the models they have on their books.

Young girls looking to break into modelling are easy prey for rip-off merchants, so make sure you get as much information as possible about any agency you go to see and, where possible, take someone with you.

# getting noticed

Getting spotted is one of the most usual ways to enter the business. All agencies use 'scouts', whose job is to traipse the streets looking for new talent. You can get spotted anytime and anywhere. Models have been spotted on planes, in clubs, at school and shopping in the high street.

The *Clothes Show* exhibition that takes place every December at the NEC in Birmingham is a prime scouting location because it attracts many young girls who are interested in fashion.

If someone approaches you and asks to take your picture, get their details and the name of the agency they represent. Don't give out personal details until you've checked that they represent a reputable agency.

Even if you're spotted you must bear in mind that for every hundred people who are scouted on the street only a couple will be taken on by an agency.

# supermodels – how they got started

Every supermodel has to start somewhere. So how did some of the world's most beautiful women get their lucky break?

**NAOMI CAMPBELL** Discovered at fifteen when an Elite agent spotted her walking down a street in Covent Garden.
**KATE MOSS** Kate was at JFK airport waiting for a flight back to England after a holiday in the Bahamas when she was spotted by Sarah Doucas from Storm.
**BRIDGET HALL** Bridget began her modelling career at the age of nine working for catalogues. She moved on to become the Guess? girl and the rest is history.
**CHRISTY TURLINGTON** Spotted at the age of thirteen riding horseback, near her home in Miami, by leading fashion photographer Dennie Cody.
**GISELE BUNDCHEN** First spotted at the age of fourteen, eating a Big Mac with her classmates whilst on a school trip. She entered the Elite model competition and came fourth.
**AMBER VALETTA** Her mother enrolled her in a modelling school at fifteen. A local agency then sent her to Milan where she did her first editorial for Italian *Vogue*.
**CLAUDIA SCHIFFER** Claudia was celebrating a friend's birthday in a Dusseldorf nightclub when an agent from Metropolitan noticed her. Two years later, she was on the cover of *Cosmo*.
**HEIDI KLUM** Heidi entered a modelling competition called Model 92 in Munich and won – as simple as that!

So, the next time you're waiting at Crewe station, just think: it may be your turn to get spotted...

## top ten tips on
## how to break into modelling

1. Get a few good snapshots of yourself. Ask a friend or relative who is handy with a camera to take them
2. Check out a few agencies and make contact
3. Be persistent. You can't expect to get taken on at the first agency you see
4. Look good. Make sure you are well groomed, dressed simply and wearing the minimum of make-up before visiting an agency
5. Do your homework. Learn all you can about the industry and what to expect
6. Stay safe. Take a friend, or a parent, if you're under eighteen, to go to any auditions or photo-shoots
7. Be professional. It is essential to be polite, businesslike and punctual whenever you meet an agent, client or go to a photoshoot
8. Be realistic. For every girl that is selected to be a model, a thousand have been rejected
9. Keep fit. You have to look after yourself if you want to be taken seriously. A model's body is her working asset
10. Learn to love yourself. We're all unique and beautiful for it. Appreciate what is good about you, and don't try to be someone you're not

## stagethree

# getting *through*

Five potential supermodels have been selected to move to the capital, sign with Premier for three months and dip their pedicured toes into the shark-infested waters of the fashion world. What will life really be like living away from family and friends, partying with the rich and famous and adopting a healthy eating and exercise regime, all while learning how to be a professional model?

The *Model Behaviour* apartment.

## Moving Day
### Thursday 28 June 2001

The final five are through: Alicia, Chermaine, Elizabeth, Maisie and Patricia. Today they move into the fashionable *MB* apartment in London's Docklands. All are apprehensive, since they don't know each other very well at all. In twenty-four hours' time they'll be living together – some sharing a room and bunk beds. As they bid their families a final farewell, the girls wonder what life will be like away from their loved ones. 'I'll really miss my little brother. I'll miss my sister. Me and my sister do everything together, so it will be hard not having her next to me,' says Patricia. Alicia is unconcerned about life away from Sheffield as she is the only one of the five who has already left home, 'I live in a shared flat, so I'm not dreading anything. I'm really looking forward to it.' Chermaine says an emotional goodbye to her boyfriend and promises not to cry. An upbeat Maisie is very positive about the prospect of life in the apartment: 'I am excited about meeting the others and seeing what the flat will be like.' For her part, Elizabeth is keen to get to London and have new experiences: 'I want to meet new people, especially famous people, and I want to be famous myself.'

The girls are knocked out when they walk into the new apartment. 'Wow!' says Maisie, as Alicia claps her hands in delight and Elizabeth declares that she could

definitely live here for three months. The apartment is brand new, very modern and overlooks the Thames Basin. The girls will have to share rooms, so they decide to draw straws. The London girls, Patricia and Chermaine, end up together and Alicia, Elizabeth and Maisie take the other room. As the girls unpack their belongings, Chermaine starts by pinning up a selection of cards from her family and friends: 'I'm putting these up so if I want to go home I can look at them and not want to.'

Later that evening, Angus Munro arrives to see if the girls have settled in, and is given a tour by Alicia. He spies a row of numerous pairs of shoes and is horrified to learn they all belong to her. 'That's obscene,' he laughs. He then chats to Patricia about her skin, and explains why she won't be going on castings with the other girls. 'I don't want to send you out to castings until you've seen a dermatologist and you've got perfect skin,' he tells her, frankly.

As the girls are all eighteen or under, they are assigned a chaperone/nanny called Rafah Sabbagh. Rafah has plenty of experience working with both teenagers and models – in fact, she used to be a model herself. Her job was to make sure that the girls abided by all the house rules – and there were plenty, but more of that later – and to teach them body work using Pilates and yoga. She was also to chaperone them if they went to any parties or launches and was the person they spoke to if they had any day-to-day prob-

lems living in the apartment. 'They have relied on me most for emotional well-being,' Rafah reveals. 'I think that's where I have been most helpful.' Apart from the house rules, the girls had to get used to looking after themselves too and were given £70 a week each to cover food and personal items.

It's the end of the day and the five finalists prepare to spend their first night away from home, and they phone home to fill in their families on what the apartment is like. Alicia's boyfriend Barry seems horrified she will be sleeping in a bunk bed, while Maisie's mother is worried her daughter may like the flat so much she won't want to come home!

## Week One

Next morning it's off to meet Angus at Premier. Premier is one of the UK's leading model agencies and has over 200 girls on its books, including big names such as Naomi Campbell and Claudia Schiffer, and for the next three months it will have five more. Even for new signings like Alicia, Patricia, Chermaine, Maisie and Elizabeth, there is the prospect of earning between £50 and £10,000 per day. Angus shows the girls a 'model book', a personal record of a model's work that includes photos, tearsheets and a card. 'Your personal book has all your original pictures in it and is worth a fortune when it's full,' he emphasizes. 'You mustn't lose

Day to day living…

**'Being here in the model apartment has given me more confidence, I think.'** *Patricia*

it, as a model's book is crucial to her success.' He then shows the girls a model card and explains its use as a point of reference for potential clients: 'Your card has your photo, name, agency and measurements on it.'

He warns the girls that the three-month contract with Premier is a trial period only: 'This is your time to prove yourself and get working. Each of you has an equal chance and it is really up to you what you do with it.'

With the more serious business over, the girls hit the local supermarket with nutritionist Maryon Stewart to do the weekly shop. It will be Maryon's job to make sure the girls eat a healthy, well-balanced diet and she is well aware that it will be a challenge: 'They were hiding things like chocolate biscuits and alcohol in the trolley. It was like going out with a group from St Trinian's – it was like your worst nightmare – taking all your five children together and having them all play up.' She also tries to persuade Chermaine not to have her customary four chocolate biscuits and a cup of tea for breakfast and allows her only one packet for the whole week. Three hours and two trolleys later, after ticking off Patricia for putting beer in the trolley and Alicia for sneaking in a bar of chocolate, Maryon finally reaches the check-out. The girls aren't best pleased with Maryon being around, as Chermaine reveals: 'I think Maryon is a nice woman but I don't think anyone takes kindly to having their diet dramatically changed.' Patricia found the changes hard to accept too, 'I'm on a very strict eating plan to improve my skin. It's been very hard to change my eating habits. I've never thought about what I'm eating before.' Their feeling come as no surprise to Maryon: 'At first I think they thought I was a pain in the neck, but after a while they did come round. Patricia realized that what I am saying about her skin is actually for her own good, and if she follows my advice her skin will get better.'

> **'I missed my animals because I am so used to having them around me.'** *Maisie*

Within a couple of days Elizabeth, Chermaine and Alicia go on their first casting to *Just 17* magazine. They manage to get lost in central London and arrive thirty minutes late, tired and feet aching. After a thirty-second meeting with the Art Director, it's off to more castings at *Bliss*, *Hair* and *Looks* magazines. Alicia can't believe all the effort that has to go into such a quick meeting and Chermaine agrees: 'I never actually wanted to do modelling full time and now I've been to a casting I know why.'

While the girls are off at castings, Patricia goes to a dermatology clinic to see a skin consultant. Antibiotics prescribed by her GP have not worked, so hopefully this will sort out the problem – otherwise she faces the prospect of leaving the house. Maisie is off at a test shoot wearing only a black bikini. 'I don't feel like a model,' she says 'I just feel like me doing something stupid.' She doesn't feel so stupid when she hears that the photos will be used in a fashion exhibition at St Martins College of Art in London. 'I could get used to this,' she smiles later.

Already, life in the shared apartment has developed a few problems. Patricia returns to find washing-up, clothes and old cups and food everywhere! 'Hungry animals,' she mutters. Tidiness will prove to be a big issue for our five cover girls, as Elizabeth reveals: 'The mess is the worst. Coming into the kitchen and finding cereal bowls with milk in them two days old is irritating, especially if I end up cleaning them up. Now there is a rota of who should be doing what when.'

One of Rafah's jobs is to smooth over any rifts between the girls and make sure they are happy. At the weekly house meeting, Alicia wishes to make a complaint about food. 'Generally I get the arse-end of everything,' she moans. 'I go to get a cookie, there's one left, I go to get a crisp, there's one left. People have to remember we are all paying equal amounts and I get the dregs.' Patricia responds, 'You just aren't quick enough. We aren't trying to starve you.' Alicia isn't impressed and wants to buy her own food. Patricia stalks off downstairs to her room, leaving Alicia grumbling to herself. It may be the first disagreement, but it won't be the last...

### Week Two

To be a cover girl, the girls need pictures, so it's been decided by Premier that they should have a test shoot. After being made up, styled and photographed, the girls await Angus's feedback. He is not impressed.

> ## 'Living with four other girls is the hardest thing.'
> ### *Alicia*

'I'm not pleased with these,' he tells Elizabeth. 'You have to look in the mirror and practise your pose to see what works best.' Elizabeth isn't surprised – she didn't like them either. To Chermaine, Angus says, 'It's not a good result.' But he's mainly unhappy with the styling and make-up, and Chermaine is happy with his feedback – 'He says my pictures were good and that I should be proud of salvaging what I did.' Maisie gets a pasting too, but again it's the styling and make-up that comes in for most criticism. 'I'm disappointed because the pictures aren't very good, but I don't know whether that's them or me,' she muses. On the positive side, Alicia's pictures are a success, and Angus compliments her – 'You come across well on camera.' 'That's good, because he thinks I'm a minger in real life,' laughs Alicia. Surprisingly, despite her skin problem, Patricia comes out the best in the photos. 'The camera really likes you. The poses are really modern and you look fantastic,' says Angus, warmly. That said, it's obvious the girls have a lot more to do if they are to make it as professional models.

It's 8.30am and Patricia's been up since 7.00am to be ready in plenty of time for her first casting. The only problem is, the others are running late. 'I hate you people,' she moans. After arriving at the casting for designer Damaris's latest collection of lingerie, Patricia and Elizabeth are selected as models to help Damaris decide if they are the type of girls she is looking for to launch the underwear at London Fashion Week. Damaris is impressed with Elizabeth – 'She is delicate and beautiful, perfect for my underwear' – but Elizabeth will have to wait up to six weeks before she knows whether she will be booked. Later that evening, Alicia is invited to an over-eighteens party, much to seventeen-year-old Patricia's annoyance. As Alicia heads off to let her hair down, the other four girls prepare for another boring night in. Alicia's night turns out to be anything but boring – she manages to blag her way in to interview Huey from the Fun Lovin' Criminals.

Two days later, Chermaine has a call-back to *19* magazine for a second casting and the others arrive at Premier for a casting with photographer Jenny Hands. After seeing the four girls, Jenny calls Maisie back in and asks her to remove her shoes. 'If they don't want me because I'm short, then there's nothing I can do

Patricia

about that and maybe I'm in the wrong job,' Maisie sighs. Jenny tells Angus that Maisie is just too short for fashion shoots – no clothes would fit her tiny frame.

It's 6.00pm and the girls hear they're off to a celebrity bash at the opening of a hotel in Trafalgar Square with judge Lorraine Candy. Alicia rummages through Patricia and Chermaine's clothes without asking to find something to wear – and it's not the first time! Patricia is not impressed. A few hours later, the girls roll back to the flat, having had a great evening – Patricia is particularly chuffed, having met Goldie.

Next morning, Rafah organizes a meditation session for the girls – cause for much amusement, particularly for Chermaine. It won't be long, though, before the merriment turns to misery, as the girls discover that Angus is coming to give them some very bad news…

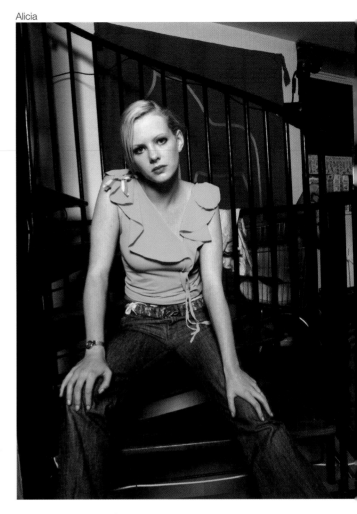

Alicia

## Week Three

The girls have been in the apartment for three weeks and have bonded well, despite the controlled regime. 'The structure of the house is really quite strict,' admits Rafah. 'It was hard for the girls, as they had to cope with an awful lot of changes all at once. They were adjusting to everything – being away from their loved ones, their friends, getting used to living in a house with so many rules and maybe even living away from home for the first time ever.' 'I had never, ever lived away from home,' confesses Chermaine. 'We live in a pub and I've a big family, so it's like [having] a really active social life. The first two weeks after moving into the apartment I got really depressed and fed up.' Family is clearly important to the girls. 'I really miss my sister,' admits Patricia. 'We've never been apart before and we're really close. I talk to her a lot by telephone.' Only Maisie found it easy: 'I wasn't too bad being away from home, because I used to go to boarding school.'

Being filmed twenty-four hours a day, seven days a week, isn't easy either, though the girls have got used to being watched. 'The cameras aren't a problem at all. At first I was, "Oh my God, the cameras,"' admits Alicia. 'You do get used to it. [But] every now and again you'll do something like pick your nose and think, "Oh my God, that's on camera!"'

Angus is about to arrive to tell the girls that someone is about to be chucked out of the apartment and have their contract with Premier terminated – and, as usual, the cameras are recording… So who will be leaving the flat? And will anyone come in to replace her?

> **'Chermaine had quite a temper on her and she had a go at me one day – that was a point where I nearly cried.' *Elizabeth***

# look at me!

To a model, beauty isn't just skin deep. A cover girl depends on her looks for her money so it's essential she takes care of herself to keep her physical appearance in tip-top condition. Her body is her most important asset and she has to maintain it in good working order.

In an industry where there is immense pressure to look picture perfect and keep slim, there lurks the temptation to drastically reduce food intake in order to maintain that ideal figure. Starving yourself is not the answer for two reasons: one, it seriously compromises your health; and two, there is no such thing as a perfect body. We are all different and learning to accept our body shape for what it is, and making the most of what we have, is essential for good self-esteem and happiness. Healthy means beautiful!

What most people don't realize is that the photos of models we see in magazines are heavily retouched to remove every tiny imperfection, wrinkle or bulge. Nobody could possibly look that good. If you've any ambition to be a model, you have to have confidence in how you look. And even if you don't have cover girl ambitions, you should have confidence in yourself. Face up to your imperfections, and remember, it's the person inside that counts. As we age our looks may fade, but our personality and our mind don't.

## healthy eating

Contrary to popular belief, most models are not anorexic or on constant diets. They eat chips, chocolate and pizza, just like the rest of us, and remain slim. Their secret is simple — only eat junk food in moderation and keep to a healthy lifestyle. Most models have healthy diets because they have to, and because it's the nature of the fashion business, although it's very hard to eat sensibly when you're constantly on the move. So if you want to improve your chances of getting a career in fashion modelling, start by changing what you eat. In fact, for your own well-being you should adopt a healthy lifestyle whether you want to be a train driver or a beauty therapist!

If you stuff your face with packets of crisps, burgers, chips and sweets daily, then you're not eating nutritiously. You are what you eat, so wouldn't you rather be more like a beautiful fresh pineapple than half a dead cow and chips? Follow *Model Behaviour*'s healthy eating plan to maintain a weight that's right for you and glow with vigorous health.

- Begin the day with a healthy breakfast to kick-start your metabolism – wholesome muesli, fruit and yoghurt is ideal
- Eat regularly – four or five small meals are metabolized more efficiently than two or three large meals
- Keep portions a sensible size. For example, instead of consuming the equivalent of Moby Dick, eat a 4oz portion of fish with some rice and salad, and try some fresh fruit afterwards
- Increase the amount of fruit and vegetables you eat to at least five portions a day
- Snack on raw vegetables, fresh fruit, seeds or nuts if you need an energy boost between meals. Grazing on vegetables throughout the day keeps your metabolism going steady
- Steer clear of alcohol, and reduce drinks that contain caffeine, like coffee, tea and cola. Fizzy drinks are heaving with calories and bad for your teeth too
- Don't eat a big meal less than three hours before going to bed, as it will be slow to metabolize
- Make sure you eat a selection of foods from the main food groups – carbohydrates (pasta, potatoes, bread), proteins (fish, cheese, meat and pulses) and vegetables

Nutritionist Maryon Stewart, who advised the *Model Behaviour* finalists on healthy eating, says many young people have nutritional deficiencies that can have devastating effects on the body, both physically and mentally: 'I see a lot of people who have health problems like PMS, migraines or general aches and pains. I show them the link between looking and feeling good and meeting your body's nutritional needs.'

**'Once you start eating healthily you don't actually want to eat junk food again.'** *Maryon Stewart – Nutritionist, Women's Nutritional Advisory Service (WNAS)*

Maryon gave each of the five finalists a healthy eating plan that was tailored to their individual needs: 'All the girls ate fast food and not one ate what I would consider a healthy diet. My first goal was to get them to eat a healthy breakfast – ideally some wholemeal muesli with fruit and yoghurt or milk.' The girls were also encouraged to eat healthy snacks of nuts or fruit rather than chocolate, crisps or cakes: 'For lunch I recommended they had something like a jacket potato with salad or a wholesome salad sandwich.' Dinner was some form of protein like meat or fish or nuts with lots of fresh vegetables and fruit: 'At first they thought I was a pain in the neck, but I think they now are seeing the effects of eating healthily and realize they need to take responsibility for themselves in order to be successful.'

Maryon is adamant that adopting healthy eating is not the same as dieting, and any weight loss happens as a by-product of eating better food: 'The evidence is strong that yo-yo dieting doesn't work. When you go on a diet your metabolic rate slows down and once you return to a normal food intake you put on weight because your metabolic rate has slowed down.' Though the pressure may be to look thin for photographic purposes, Maryon says it is important to stay healthy: 'My role is to ensure the girls are healthy and knowledge-able about their bodies' nutritional needs and how to meet them. If you want to lose weight it is better to do exercise at least four times a week to speed up your metabolic rate and tone up your muscles.'

Above all, remember, your aim is to maintain the ideal weight for your age and height. If you eat a balanced diet and exercise regularly, this shouldn't be too difficult. While it's true that models are generally slim, it's worth noting that most are very young, and at a young age most of us tend to be a lot slimmer than when we get older. And if you have big bones, you will always look bigger than someone with a petite frame, no matter how much weight you lose.

> **'I prefer to see women who look strong and fit rather than women who are really thin.'**
> *Chris St. George - Fitness instructor, Third Space*

## pumpin' iron

Exercise is an important part of maintaining a healthy lifestyle, but it doesn't necessarily mean you have to spend hours down the gym. Any cardiovascu-lar activity (cycling, swimming, running etc.) for half an hour three or four times a week will make you look better and feel better too. Exercise not only helps to keep the body toned, it also alleviates stress and increases stamina.

A combination of exercises that increase your heart rate, aid stretching and toning and increase your strength are perfect for the gruelling schedules that are all part of a model's daily life. The *Model Behaviour* girls were given membership to London's exclusive gym Third Space, and fitness instructor Chris St. George

> **'I do enjoy going to the gym because I am noticing the results now. My stomach is really toned.'**
> *Alicia*

provided them with a fitness programme to improve their strength and stamina. 'I did a day of fitness testing and analysis to determine their strength, cardiovascular capacity, flexibility, body fat, lung function etc to get a general picture of their health and fitness levels. I then wrote fitness programmes tailored to each of them,' explains Chris.

The girls were then put through their paces with fitness plans that coupled cardiovascular exercise (cycling, running and cross-training) to improve their heart and lungs and burn fat with strength training (repeti-tions using light weights) to improve their muscle tone. 'The girls do high repetitions so they don't increase muscle bulk but improve muscle strength and tone instead,' says Chris, who trains big-name sporting professionals.

According to Chris, it isn't essential you join a gym to get fit: 'When you are young you should follow an active regime like walking, swimming or cycling. When you get older you can either do some fitness training on a regular basis at a gym or even get into a hobby like climbing, swimming or martial arts.' One thing is for certain - you aren't going to get fit lying in front of the TV scoffing popcorn!

## chillin' out

Modelling can take its toll on you both mentally and physically. To combat the stresses and strains associated with life in the limelight you should take time out to relax and regain your balance. Yoga is a fantastic way to tone your body and relax your mind. Yoga allows the mind and body to work in harmony, improving posture, strength and breathing. Many models take up yoga – Christy Turlington never goes anywhere without her yoga mat.

Meditation is another tremendously useful way to unwind. All you need is a quiet area and a mantra that you can chant to yourself over and over again. The aim is to calm your mind, ridding it of everyday rubbish and worries, enabling it to focus on something that is important to you. Many people find working out or listening to music just as relaxing – the important thing is to do what is right for you.

Most importantly of all, you must get plenty of sleep. Late nights mean dull eyes, black rings and lifeless skin and hair for starters. Constant lack of sleep leads to poor health, bad attitudes and unprofessional timekeeping – not the best qualities to be a successful model, or indeed a professional of any kind. You need your beauty sleep, so get to bed early whenever you can – it's a habit you'll be grateful for later.

After investing time and effort adopting a healthy lifestyle and producing *your* perfect body, don't be tempted to cover it all up when visiting an agency or going for your test shoot. Agents are interested in the genuine package – that's what makes you unique. Wear simple clothing – nothing too baggy or too tight. Wear something that's comfortable and shows off your figure. Don't pile on the slap – wear little or no make-up. An agent wants to see you looking natural. Your hair should be simple too, and nails manicured and unvarnished.

You're feeling good and looking good, so now it's time to go see an agency...

# *top ten* health tips

1. **DON'T SMOKE** If you smoke, you're damaging your looks as well as your health. Apart from the risk of developing smoking-related diseases, cigarettes have a terrible effect on your skin and hair, making them dull and lifeless. Smokers tend to develop wrinkles earlier too.

2. **HEALTHY EATING** You should eat a healthy diet – plenty of fruit, salad and vegetables and lean fish or meat. Though it's tempting to snack on chocolate and biscuits to give yourself an energy boost, stick to a high-protein snack like cheese or strips of roast chicken. Or choose some fruit and sticks of raw vegetables dipped in hummus.

3. **EXERCISE** A model's body is her temple and she must keep it in shape. Twenty minutes of aerobic exercise every day keeps your heart and body healthy.

4. **DRINK PLENTY OF WATER** Eight glasses a day should keep the doctor away. Water acts as a great internal cleanser, flushing away all those toxins we build up in our bodies.

5. **CHILL OUT** It's important to relax when you can. Modelling is fast-paced and when on a job a model can be on her feet for up to sixteen hours. So make sure you give yourself time to unwind doing something that suits you, whether it be yoga, meditation, listening to music or taking up dance classes.

6. **PAMPER YOURSELF** When you have a packed schedule, it is essential to make time to treat yourself. Have a facial, manicure or massage. Or go and see family and friends.

7. **HAVE REGULAR CHECK-UPS** Your health is your most important asset – regular visits to your doctor and dentist will ensure that any minor problems are picked up early and don't develop into anything more serious.

8. **AVOID ALCOHOL** Booze is dehydrating and fattening, two no-nos as far as maintaining a healthy, clear complexion and perfect body are concerned.

9. **GET GROOMED** A model must turn up to a job looking well groomed, which means regular manicures and pedicures, good-condition, well-cut tresses and a pearly white smile.

10. **WALK TALL** Posture is very important in modelling. Have you ever seen a fashion model slouch down the catwalk, shoulders hunched and head down? No, neither have we. Stand in front of a full-length mirror to check how you hold your body and correct any slouch.

# alicia bostock

- Height: 5'8"
- Bust: 34"
- Waist: 25"
- Hips: 34.5"
- Shoe size: 5
- Eyes: Green
- Hair: Blonde
- Style: Feisty, sassy
- Age: 19
- Lives: Sheffield
- Family: Mum and fiancé Barry
- Fave store: Selfridges
- Fave animals: Cats and rabbits
- Fave colour: Purple
- Fave film: *True Romance*
- Worst habit: Short temper
- Best feature: Shoulders
- Worst feature: Bottom
- Best-kept secret: 'People think emotionally and mentally that I'm hard, but I'm not!'
- Never be seen dead in: New Look
- Must-have make-up: Body lotion – 'It's like foundation for legs.'
- Can't live without: Heels
- Ambition: 'Just to be really sorted.'

Fiercely independent and very single minded, Alicia may appear to be a tough northern lass on the outside, but on the inside she's a bit of a softie. Not very many people get to see that side of her, though! Alicia's addicted to shoes, and has a collection to rival that of Imelda Marcos. She has always been well into fashion and makes her own clothes, and if the right opportunities come along, she won't say no to a modelling career. In ten years time she'd like to be living in a cottage in the country with boyfriend Barry and a daughter – little Maisie Allen!

**'On the day we had to move to London into the model house I sat in the shower and cried my eyes out.'**

*Alicia on Alicia:* **'I am aggressive, exciting, fun, caring, hard-faced and honest.'**

# elizabeth creightmore

## 'I don't think fame will go to my head – I hope it doesn't.'

- ✿ Height: 5'9.5"
- ✿ Bust: 33"
- ✿ Waist: 25"
- ✿ Hips: 35"
- ✿ Shoe size: 6
- ✿ Eyes: Brown
- ✿ Hair: Dark brown
- ✿ Style: Mischievous, exotic
- ✿ Age: 16
- ✿ Lives: Forest Row, East Sussex
- ✿ Family: Foster Mum, Mum and Dad
- ✿ Fave fashion item: 'A camouflage shirt I just bought with loads of badges on it.'
- ✿ Fave store: Top Shop
- ✿ Fave animal: 'I love all animals – to eat and to cuddle!'
- ✿ Fave colour: Black
- ✿ Fave film: *Nuts in May*.
- ✿ Fave music: 'I like soundtracks.'
- ✿ Worst habit: 'Snoring when I've got my brace in.'
- ✿ Best feature: Neck
- ✿ Worst feature: Eyebags
- ✿ Never be seen dead in: A bright purple suit
- ✿ Must-have make-up: Eyeliner
- ✿ Can't live without: 'All my *League of Gentlemen* stuff.'
- ✿ Ambition: 'To be famous.'

Elizabeth is both the youngest and the craziest of the group. Despite appearing as cool as a cucumber, she has a wicked sense of humour and a sharp-witted tongue to match. She's besotted with TV show *The League of Gentlemen* and won't go anywhere without her LOG merchandise. She has always wanted to be famous, and will try acting if modelling doesn't work out. Elizabeth is a real country girl, loves animals and could never be parted from her horse. She might consider moving on if she could to go to Africa and work with chimps, though.

**Elizabeth on Elizabeth: 'I would say I am ambitious, optimistic, creative – I love drawing – and calm. I'm an easy-going person and I just want to get on with everyone. To come into an environment where there are lots of arguments I found quite a shock.'**

# chermaine murphy

- ❋ Height: 5'7.5"
- ❋ Bust: 34"
- ❋ Waist: 25"
- ❋ Hips: 35"
- ❋ Shoe size: 5
- ❋ Eyes: brown
- ❋ Hair: brown
- ❋ Style: Sparky, studious
- ❋ Qualifications: 9 straight-A AS levels
- ❋ Ambition: 'To study English at university.'
- ❋ Age: 17
- ❋ Lives: East London
- ❋ Family: Mum. Dad, six sisters
- ❋ Fave model: Naomi Campbell
- ❋ Fave fashion item: Jeans
- ❋ Fave store: Prada
- ❋ Best kept secret: I can't tell you
- ❋ Fave colour: Pink
- ❋ Fave film: *Pretty in Pink*
- ❋ Fave CD: *Dirty Dancing*
- ❋ Never be seen dead in: A pair of Reebok classics
- ❋ Most embarrassing moment: Dancing in one of the castings
- ❋ Must have make-up: Mascara
- ❋ Can't live without: Pictures of my family and friends
- ❋ Would most like to change: My feet, because I've a foot phobia
- ❋ Worst habit: I can be quite outspoken
- ❋ Worst feature: My eyes are too far apart
- ❋ Best feature: I've got a big joker smile

Chermaine is an East End girl who lives in a pub – but she's no Sharon Watts. With beauty and brains, Chermaine has nine straight-A AS levels and she's hoping to gain a place at Kings College London University next year to read English. With a tongue that could cut ice, she admits she can be a 'very outspoken', and her Mum says she 'does not suffer fools gladly.' But one flash of that big wide grin and she's forgiven. Chermaine loves fashion and designer clothes, and admits to being spoilt by her Mum and her boyfriend. She's only ever wanted to be happy in life and finish her education, but if she can earn money modelling at the same time she'll give it her best shot.

**Chermaine on Chermaine:**
**'I am very, very confident (some people might say egotistical but I'm not), funny, friendly, outgoing, a bit of a cow, oh, and intelligent.'**

**'The whole thing has been a learning experience.'**

# jenny richards

- Height: 5'8"
- Bust: 32"
- Waist: 23.5"
- Hips: 32"
- Shoe size: 5
- Eyes: Blue
- Hair: Pale blonde
- Style: Edgy, feminine
- Age: 18
- Lives: Newport, Wales
- Family: Mum, partner Craig and daughter Lacey (aged 2)
- Fave fashion item: Jeans
- Fave store: Top Shop
- Fave film: *Kevin and Perry Go Large In Ibiza*
- Fave hair product: L'Oréal conditioner
- Fave pop group: The Corrs
- Fave film star: Bruce Willis
- Worst habit: None
- Best feature: Legs
- Worst feature: Ears
- Must-have make-up: Fake tan
- Can't live without: Lacey; mobile phone
- Ambition: 'To be a model and build a better life for my family.'

**'I do think about fame and being a supermodel because I really do want it.'**

Rejected at the end of Workshop Week, Jenny was completely gutted as she is desperate to become a professional model. She couldn't believe her luck when she was told she'd been given a second chance as Maisie's replacement. Joining three weeks after the other girls, she was determined to make her mark even though it was heart-wrenching to leave her two year-old daughter Lacey at home in Newport, Wales, with partner Craig. With long legs to die for and beautiful blonde looks, Jenny really wants to use her assets to build a better future for her family.

*Jenny on Jenny:* **'I am easily upset by comments. I am coping with the whole thing quite well. I am a terrible person for crying. I just can't help it.'**

# patricia sheehan

- ✺ Height: 5'7"
- ✺ Bust: 34"
- ✺ Waist: 24"
- ✺ Hips: 36"
- ✺ Shoe size: 6
- ✺ Eyes: Brown
- ✺ Hair: Brown
- ✺ Style: Cool, mysterious
- ✺ Age: 17
- ✺ Lives: South-east London
- ✺ Family: Mum, Dad, three sisters and a brother.
- ✺ Fave model: Kate Moss
- ✺ Fave fashion item: Jeans
- ✺ Fave shop: Top Shop
- ✺ Fave animal: Horse
- ✺ Fave colour: Green
- ✺ Fave film: *Romeo and Juliet* or *Braveheart*
- ✺ Fave pop group: Bon Jovi
- ✺ Worst habit: Moaning
- ✺ Best feature: Eyes
- ✺ Worst feature: Thighs
- ✺ Must-have make-up: Liquid eyeliner
- ✺ Can't live without: Liquid eyeliner
- ✺ Ambition: 'To be an artist.'

Patricia is half Irish and lives in Deptford in south-east London. Good looks run in the family as Patricia's mother was once a model and Patricia has a classic Audrey Hepburn look. Though she's quite shy, she showed amazing courage in baring a bad case of acne to the world in her bid to become a model, and is known for speaking her mind. She is optimistic about overcoming her skin condition and has changed her diet drastically to make sure it improves. She is a bit of an artist and her ambition is to illustrate children's books. If she makes it as a model, her sister reckons she should get 50 per cent of her earnings as she's the one that pushed her to enter *Model Behaviour*!

**Patricia on Patricia:**
**'I'm really shy, I am a bit moany and can be miserable. I'm also snappy, impatient, caring, nice usually, good fun and sarcastic.'**

# maisie waller

- Height: 5'5"
- Bust: 32"
- Waist: 24"
- Hips: 34"
- Shoe size: 6
- Eyes: Blue
- Hair: Brown
- Style: Cheeky, earthy
- Age: 17
- Lives: New Forest, Hampshire
- Family: Mum, Dad and brother (aged 14)
- Hero: Lara Croft
- Animals: Dogs, cats, rabbits and her horse called Willie
- Fave fashion item: 'Anything that makes me feel good and that I look good in.'
- Fave store: Kookai
- Fave film: *Silence of the Lambs*
- Fave colour: Blue
- Fave pop group: 'I like loads of stuff.'
- Worst habit: 'Moaning and putting myself down.'
- Best feature: Eyes
- Worst feature: Height
- Never be seen dead in: 'A Jeep, because I love Land Rover.'
- Must-have make-up: Kohl
- Can't live without: 'Photos of my animals.'
- Ambition: 'To be successful at whatever I do.'

**Maisie on Maisie: 'I am quite quiet and withdrawn until I get to know people. I can be quite fun and funny. I do have low self-esteem and put myself down which I think really annoys some people.'**

**'I never thought I was pretty enough to be a model, but everyone told me I should try.'**

Maisie's natural look suits her natural lifestyle – she lives deep in the New Forest surrounded by her animals, and loves to spend time horse-riding and driving her Landrover cross-country to school. Lara Croft is her hero and she is a keen member of the Cadets. Maisie never thought she was pretty enough to be a model, but she's in no doubt now that her looks are every bit as attractive as her sunny personality. She has only one ambition in life, and that's to be successful in whatever she chooses to do.

# it's in the
# bag...

Apart from her portfolio, a model's single most important possession is her model bag, which contains everything she needs to look flawless and feel confident. Check out *Model Behaviour*'s guide to the essential modelling kit to keep you looking gorgeous.

## MODEL BAG

You'll need a good quality bag in which to carry your essential modelling gear. It needs to be roomy enough to accommodate a portfolio and hard-wearing too – you'll take it everywhere with you!

## MAKE-UP BAG

Modelling and make-up go hand-in-hand, so you'll never be far away from your face paint. Again, invest in a good quality bag that will stand up to tough treatment.

## MOBILE PHONE

The fashion industry is a fast-moving one. Details of a job can alter right up to the last minute, so a model must be contactable at all times. A mobile phone is an absolute essential for keeping up to date with plans... and for having a gossip with your friends and family when you're waiting around for the next casting!

## A MAGAZINE OR BOOK

It can get very tedious waiting around at castings and photoshoots, so it's a good idea to carry something to read to stave off boredom. If you aren't a bookworm, take a Walkman instead.

## BOTTLED WATER

Water is a model's best friend. It's great for detox and you should be drinking eight glasses a day to keep your skin clear and healthy.

## PORTFOLIO

Don't leave home without it! A model's portfolio is a personal record of her career. If she's just starting out it contains all her test shots and model cards. As she does more work, it'll start to feature more Polaroids and photos from actual jobs. Models can be called to a casting at any time, so they must always have their portfolio on them.

## WORK PLANNER

Models have busy schedules that they must manage themselves. They have to turn up for a job or 'go-see' at the right place and the right time. Being 'fashionably late' doesn't figure in a model's work – not if she wants to be seen as a professional, anyway. Her work planner (either a diary or a personal organizer) contains all her appointments and contacts.

## PASSPORT

If you are planning to model professionally, you could be on the other side of the world within a few hours, so it's important to be prepared.

# beauty *is* skin deep

A beauty regime is a must for any aspiring model, so if you don't do so already, get yourself a daily cleanse, tone and moisturize routine. Don't flop into bed with your war paint on – no matter how late it is. Remove every last trace of make-up, to keep your skin looking clear and healthy.

Most models have their own personal favourite products that suit their skin and their personality, and it's up to you to find products that suit you and your purse! Skincare products don't have to be expensive – baby cream can work just as well as a cleanser!

If you've adopted a healthy eating plan and are cleansing, toning and moisturizing daily, your skin should be trouble free. If you do get a dreaded spot the night before a casting – or a hot date, for that matter – use concealer to banish the blemish.

Skin is vital to the success of a model's career. Your skin is the best advert for your inner health and vitality. Whatever your skin type, on the whole it needs to naturally clear for you to be a successful model, and even if you don't plan to be a model, clear skin gives you confidence in your looks. There are models that suffer from skin problems such as acne, eczema or psoriasis, and if you have a skin disorder you should make an appointment with a dermatologist (skin specialist) who'll be able to advise you on the best treatment. Patricia has relatively bad acne, but that didn't stop her getting

> **'I see pretty faces every day. Beauty is not just something you are born with – you have to learn to love yourself, care for your body and find inner peace.'**
> *Carole White, Director of Premier Model Management*

through to the final five and she's now trying to do something about it: 'I'm on a strict eating plan to improve my skin. I'm sticking to it really well even though it's been hard to change my eating habits.' As nutritionist Maryon Stewart points out, many young people don't realize that what they eat affects their health and well-being: 'Patricia didn't realize that all the burgers and chocolate she ate had an effect on her skin. But she's now realized that if she follows my advice her skin will get better, which is what has happened.'

To keep your skin healthy and young looking, you should moisturize both from the outside and the inside, which means drinking plenty of water – at least eight glasses a day. If you really can't bear to drink water on its own, then add some low-sugar squash or a little fresh fruit juice to give it a lift. The other essential ingredient to keep skin looking clear and healthy is sleep. Skip on your snoozing and it'll soon show on your face – dark rings, sagging eyelids and grey skin – not very attractive!

# getting the look

The *Model Behaviour* finalists all have very different complexions, as make-up artist Mark Cook, who prepared the girls for their Workshop Week photos, reveals: 'Jenny has fair, translucent skin so you have to be careful of the colour you use. Keep it as close to your natural skin tone as possible. I used a Stila sports base that is very natural. Patricia has quite fair skin even though she is dark-haired, so I could get away with a lot more colour. I applied concealer with a brush to cover the blemishes and used a strong lipstick. Alicia has a yellow tone to her skin and has a very good complexion. She can take a lot of different looks – natural or glamorous. Elizabeth has quite short lashes, so she always lines her eyes. She had a good complexion too. I smudged the eyeliner to open the eye out and make it look softer.'

The girls also have different taste in make-up. 'I don't really wear much make-up,' admits Jenny, 'but I am a real fan of body creams and all that pampering stuff.' Alicia, on the other hand, loves make-up but can be a bit naughty on the cleansing front: 'I've got really sensitive skin and I find Dior the best – you don't have to take it off at night!' Maisie loves her kohl but confesses she never buys expensive products: 'I hate spending money!' Patricia suffers with her complexion, so she never goes anywhere without her concealer, although she admits that 'I really can't live without my liquid eyeliner' too! Elizabeth loves make-up, but is choosy about what she buys: 'I don't agree with wearing make-up that has been tested on animals.' Chermaine doesn't wear much make-up, 'but I have to have mascara on.'

Make-up is a very personal thing. What suits you depends on so many factors – your skin type, colouring, lifestyle and even your personality. Whether you want to be a model or not, it's worth learning as much as you can about make-up and its application. The aim of using make-up is to enhance, not detract, from your natural beauty, something Mark Cook agrees with: 'My style is natural beauty. I enhance people's beauty rather than use a lot of make-up. You don't have to wear every bit of make-up – you just end up putting on too much. If you're young, all you really need is a tinted moisturizer or light base, some mascara and maybe a duotone, which is a lipstick, blusher and eyeshadow all-in-one.'

The first step is to examine your face free of make-up. Look at your skin colour, your eye shape, your lips, your hair colour and the shapes of your brow, your cheekbones, face etc. Experiment with different shades of eye-colour, blush and lipstick. See what works for you. You can test different make-up without spending a fortune – just go to your local chemist or the cosmetic counter of your nearest department store and try the testers. Body Shop and Superdrug are great for browsing and trying out make-up. Salespeople will often do a trial make-up session free of charge too.

Does red lipstick make you look tarty, or glamorous? Is blue eyeshadow your colour, or do you look better in more earthy tones? Once you discover what works for you, buy yourself a selection of good quality make-up (again, this doesn't have to be expensive), and some decent make-up brushes. You'll need an eyeshadow brush, a big fluffy blusher brush, a lip brush, a brow brush, an eyeliner brush and a sponge to apply foundation. 'Get a little bag first and slowly add things to it as you get your pocket money each week,' advises Mark. 'You do need brushes – a lip brush is very important.'

Depending on the look you want to create, you may choose only to wear a selection of the above make-up for a more natural look, or go the whole hog for a glam evening. 'You should save wearing strong colours of lipstick and shadows for the evening,' says Mark. 'Just by changing your lipstick you can change the look. You can alter your face dramatically by altering the way you apply make-up. You can do strong eyes and leave lips natural, or natural eyes and strong lips.'

## making up

Mark Cook says applying make-up is all about experimenting: 'If you've got an idea, try it. Make-up isn't permanent, so if you don't like it, just wash it off. Try out products.' Make-up should be applied in a set order: foundation or base, concealer, loose powder (if you need it), eyeshadow, eyeliner, mascara, eyebrow colour, blush and lipstick. How much you apply, and whether you slap on everything, depends on the image you want to create.

Mark has this advice on how to apply make-up, though he agrees it's a very personal thing: 'Start with a base – either tinted moisturizer or light foundation. Use it to even everything out, not cover up. Any blemishes like spots or dark rings should be covered using concealer. Don't use too much, as it draws attention, and make sure you use the right colour for your skin. Then apply eyeshadow, liner and mascara. Don't forget eyebrows. They are important because they shape your face. You can use pencil, but I use a small angled brush and eyebrow powder. I then do the lips and finish off with blusher.'

The colours you choose depend on the look you want to achieve and what suits you more than what's in fashion. This season's look is nude lips and smouldering eyes. For eyes, use charcoal liners and black or dark brown shadows smudged to give a smoky look. Lips are barely there, with a touch of natural coloured lipstick or a smear of Vaseline to give a deliciously kissable pout. But you can do what you like. 'People always ask me what the current look is, Nowadays it's all different looks and you can just pick one you like. Smoky eyes and natural lips are in now, but at the same time, so is glamour,' explains Mark.

## don't forget

Last but not least, remember your nails and hair. Nails must not be bitten to the quick, but nor should they be great long talons. A cover girl's nails should be well-manicured, buffed and polished. If you wear polish, keep it natural with a clear protective varnish. It pays to get a professional manicure once a month to keep your nails in perfect condition, or to get one of your mates to do them. Don't forget your hands either. 'Gorgeous hands, feet and skin are important. It's amazing how many girls (including top models) have terrible nails and feet,' reveals photographer Donna Francesca.

Keep your hair clean, well cut and conditioned. Banish split ends by regularly visiting your hairdresser for a trim and protect your hair from excessive drying and the sun. If you enjoy swimming, put your hair in a swimming cap to protect it from chemicals or salt water.

Ideally, you should not have your hair permed or coloured, as agents might like to see your hair in its natural state when they are auditioning you. If your hair is permed or coloured, make sure you pay particular attention to deep conditioning and have it trimmed more often. Oliver Woods, hairdresser to the stars including Jude Law, Kate Winslet and Kate Moss, gives this advice: 'To keep your hair in good condition, don't wash it too often. Washing your hair every day is a bad idea. Keep it natural and try not to do too much with it. Anthony Mascolo of Toni & Guy agrees: 'Have a good cut done every six weeks to get rid of split ends,' he advises, 'and make sure you aren't allergic to a product.'

Whether you become a model or not, looking after your skin, hair and nails and learning how to apply make-up to make the most of what you have will keep you looking your best, something you'll be thankful for later on.

## top ten tips for looking good

1. **CTM** Cleanse, tone and moisturise
2. **START SNOOZING** Get eight hours a night to keep your skin glowing and eyes sparkling
3. **DE-STRESS TRESSES** Keep your hair conditioned, well-groomed and regularly trimmed
4. **GET GLEAMING** Brush, floss and polish your teeth for a pearly white smile. Go to a dentist to sort out any problems
5. **NAIL 'EM** Pedicure and manicure regularly for perfect nails
6. **EAT HEALTHILY** You are what you eat. For good condition hair, nails and skin, eat lots of fresh fruit and vegetables
7. **REHYDRATE** Eight glasses a day keeps the doctor away and you looking sensational
8. **MAKE-UP** Learn how to apply it and what suits you best
9. **GO NATURAL** Don't be tempted to pile on the slap. Make-up is there to accentuate your best features
10. **BE HAPPY** No matter how beautiful you are, a miserable face is always unattractive

# getting*on*

Life in the *Model Behaviour* apartment isn't always fun. When five girls are thrown together, with hormones raging, personalities clashing and tempers flying, there are bound to be some fireworks.

The girls have spent three weeks in their new apartment and already there have been big upheavals. The judges have had to call an emergency meeting to discuss the fate of Maisie who, though stunningly beautiful, is proving not to have what it takes to be a model – mainly because she's only 5' 5".

All five finalists have already been on several castings, and some have been called back by the client, though none of them have had any definite bookings. Sadly, no clients so far are happy about using Maisie, simply because they think she's too short. Angus had hoped that Maisie's good looks and personality would outshine the fact that she's about three inches shorter than the average fashion model, but it just isn't working out that way.

Maisie

## Movin' Out

Angus has warned the girls he is coming to the flat to tell them that someone will be leaving. 'We knew someone was leaving because they brought it up, even though they had said they would not be reviewing us until after a month, so that came as a bit of a shock,' Maisie explains. Angus arrives and the girls are anxious to hear who is moving out, though one of them already has a pretty good idea. 'I knew it was going to be me because Angus wouldn't look at me,' Maisie recalls. 'It was quite obvious it would be me, because of my height.' 'Everyone knows why I am here,' begins Angus. 'We take on people who we think have potential, but if it doesn't work out we have to let them go. We've decided that we are going to have to tell you to leave, Maisie.' Maisie is devastated and the tears well up in her eyes, and roll down her cheeks: 'I didn't think I would cry but all of a sudden I realized I was, and I thought, "Oh no, I didn't want to do that",' she reflects later.

'I never thought I was pretty enough to be a model,' Maisie cries as she buries her head in her hands, distraught. Angus reassures her that she is indeed pretty enough – she's just not tall enough. Maisie feels she's been let down by her size: 'I never would have thought of myself as short before this, and I did not even think about my height, and now it's been brought to my attention quite severely.'

Having spent three weeks getting to know each other, the remaining four finalists are devastated to

**'It's unrealistic to put five strangers in a house together and expect them to all get on.'** *Jenny*

hear that one of their group has been rejected. 'I was really upset when Maisie left, because we had a lot in common. We were both country girls and both had horses and we were quite posh compared to the others,' reveals Elizabeth. 'When they kicked Maisie out, we had to start all over again. I was really, really upset when she left. It upset the whole dynamic of the group,' says Chermaine. So much so, that when Maisie was told she was going, life coach Gladeana was brought in to offer the girls support: 'I was asked to be there when they broke the news. It was a very, very sad situation. Everybody was quite upset.' As Maisie says an emotional farewell to her model mates, the others begin to wonder who will be chucked out next. Maisie, however, is philosophical about the whole experience as she returns to normal life, to finish the rest of her exams in January. 'I knew the risk and I took it. I still think I was right to take it,' she says, plainly. Alicia, meanwhile, isn't sure whether she's happy or disappointed that she wasn't the one being thrown out, while Chermaine definitely isn't happy about it, and is now thinking of leaving herself...

## Movin' In

The Panel are looking for a replacement for Maisie, and has a meeting to decide which of the five finalists who didn't get picked to live in the apartment would be most suitable. After making their selection, judge Lorraine

Candy gives the lucky girl in question the good news. The four flatmates already had an inkling who it might be... 'We thought it would be Jenny,' reveals Patricia. Next day, Maisie's replacement arrives, and it is indeed Jenny Richards, a nineteen-year-old mum from Newport. Jenny is desperate to be a model and is over the moon when she hears she will be living in the Model Apartment after all: 'I was gutted when I wasn't picked to move in after workshop week. When I heard three weeks later I was moving in I couldn't believe it!'

After Maisie's departure, the others feel a little resentful towards their new flatmate. They aren't impressed that Jenny had moved in after three weeks but hadn't had to suffer all the restrictions they had experienced, such as not being able to see family and friends for the first two weeks. 'Because Maisie had to go I wasn't overly enthusiastic about Jenny coming today,' admits Chermaine. 'I was depressed about Maisie, but out of the five girls I'm glad they chose Jenny because I liked her,' says Patricia. Maisie herself bears no grudges: 'I think Jenny's a lovely girl and it's really good for her.'

Jenny hasn't had an easy ride, though, as she has had to move into an established group and, hardest of all, she has had to leave her eighteen-month-old daughter Lacey behind with partner Craig. 'It is really, really hard living away from home, especially without the baby,' she confesses. 'I was apprehensive about

Elizabeth helps Jenny choose a bedroom.

moving in because the others have had three weeks to bond and because I'm Maisie's replacement. Though it's not my fault, I didn't know how they'd be about it. They've all been really nice, though.' The next day, Jenny goes to castings at Premier with the others, and her confidence impresses the model agency. Not to mention Patricia: 'She puts me to shame,' she remarks.

It's four weeks since the girls left their homes. They are having a party at the flat and have been allowed to invite members of their family and friends. First Barry (Alicia's boyfriend) and Craig (Jenny's boyfriend) arrive, followed by Patricia's sister and Elizabeth's friends. Chermaine is left waiting anxiously for boyfriend Jonathan, who finally arrives half an hour late. She is thrilled to see him, but as the time approaches for the guests to leave, the pressure of the last four weeks begins to take its toll and Chermaine begins to crack. 'It makes me angry, and anyone that says something to me again, I'm gonna have to punch them,' she shouts. 'I'm gonna have to kill someone if I can't go home.' The girl's chaperone, Rafah, goes to see if Chermaine is all right once she has calmed down. 'Chermaine's sense of well-being is really up the spout,' Rafah reveals later. 'She wanted to be with her friends and finish her course work, so it was quite hard for her. In the course of the last four weeks she has shown an inability to control her emotions – she has a lot of rage, kicking doors when things aren't to her liking.'

After much soul-searching, Chermaine decides to stay in the flat and give it her best shot, though she still has very strong reservations about the whole exercise. 'I was annoyed with myself for putting myself through this. It was never going to be a great ambition for me like it is for Jenny,' she admits. 'I thought I was completely wasting my time, as I didn't ever not want to go to university or finish my A Levels. It was so strange to get through and I wanted to know what it was like... which is why I stayed.'

## Movin' Out

The day after the party, everyone but Chermaine, who is left in bed still wondering about her future, goes on a casting and gets a new set of pictures. After taking shots of all the girls and commenting on how relaxed they are in front of the camera, photographer Jenny Hands reveals that she'd only actually consider using one of them: Elizabeth.

New arrival Jenny has wall-to-wall castings and a test shoot at the end of her first week. Having spent a day going from one casting to another, she's 'definitely wearing trainers tomorrow!' However, there's a flipside to Jenny's good fortune. Rafah thinks her successful start may be a cause of some of the problems in the house, as competition has started to set in, with some of the flatmates getting more work than others: 'The other four resent Jenny a bit,' Rafah admits, 'and it's also because she came in late but immediately got all the privileges that they had to earn.'

And it doesn't take long for the ill feelings to come to the surface. Tantrums and tears soon become a regular occurrence in the *MB* apartment. Chermaine in particular becomes more disillusioned and frustrated with life there: 'I wasn't very happy and I didn't get on with Alicia,' she says, looking back on her time in the apartment. 'She made Jenny cry and it caused a bad atmosphere for everyone else.... Jenny is sweet, but living with her became aggravating because she kept crying all the time and wouldn't stand up to Alicia.' Even laid-back Elizabeth was finding it a strain: 'Jenny and Alicia have arguments, and Jenny is quite sensitive. The worst thing is probably the fighting. I'm quite a calm person and I don't like arguments.' Patricia, who gets on with Chermaine better than the others, is aware of how unhappy her friend is: 'Chermaine is miserable here. She just wants to go home.'

At the weekly group chat with Rafah, the girls air their problems. Alicia decides to voice her opinion on living with Jenny: 'I think you moan about everything,' she states, flatly. Jenny doesn't understand what Alicia means and asks why she is having a go at her. 'Jenny, if I were having a go at you, you'd be on the floor,' Alicia retorts. Upset, Jenny escapes to her room, though Rafah wants Alicia and Jenny to talk about the issues between them. Patricia firmly believes it's the green-eyed monster at work. 'We've been here four weeks and got no work, and you've been here a week and got a photoshoot already,' she explains to Jenny. 'She's jealous.'

After five weeks and fifty castings, none of the girls have yet had paid work, but all that changes when Jenny and Patricia hear they have a firm booking to do a shoot for a Thai fashion label. 'I never expected me and Jenny to be the first to get jobs. I am really excited but a bit nervous too,' admits Patricia.

Soon all the girls except Alicia have been booked for work – Chermaine lands a job for Aveda, and Elizabeth has a shoot with *Girl About Town* magazine. Alicia is unimpressed; she decides to let the other girls (particularly Jenny) know how she feels about the mess they leave in the flat, via a series of nasty notes. Rows erupt again over housework until Rafah is forced to introduce a rota. Jenny is upset by Alicia's aggressive attitude to her, but Alicia is unrepentant: 'I don't enjoy living with you, but I don't cry about everything.' Eventually, Chermaine loses her rag and phones her mum, who races round to the flat and gives the other girls a piece of her mind!

Alicia is happier when she hears that she's going to appear in a music video for Swedish pop group

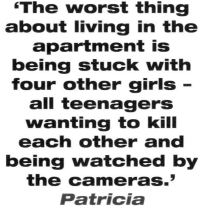

> ## 'The worst thing about living in the apartment is being stuck with four other girls – all teenagers wanting to kill each other and being watched by the cameras.'
> ### *Patricia*

Chermaine

Backyard Babies. Jenny, meanwhile, is to appear in the *Observer* Sunday supplement, which she is delighted about. With all the girls having secured work, Angus decides to call them into Premier for feedback.

The bad news for Jenny is that Kevin Ford, the *Observer* photographer, says her pictures didn't make an impact. However, Alicia, Chermaine, Patricia and Elizabeth all get reasonably good feedback considering they are beginners, and on the whole Angus is pleased.

The girls continue to go to castings, but one of them has now decided she's had enough. Chermaine feels she can't take the pressure any more. Living in the apartment has become unbearable both for her and the others because she is so unhappy, so she has come to a decision and decided to throw in the towel: 'I want to leave because I am unhappy here,' she confesses. 'Alicia winds me up to the point that I want to kill her. I want to start college on time and I want to see my friends and family.' Angus, though sad she will be leaving, is not surprised. 'I understand the education thing,' he tells her. 'I believe education is far more important than modelling and you can always come back to modelling later.'

Chermaine leaves with boyfriend Jonathan, and all the girls come out to wave her goodbye. Well, nearly all — Alicia stays indoors, despite Rafah's attempts to persuade her to come down. Patricia was distraught at Chermaine's departure, as she recalls later: 'I really wanted to go home then. It was really upsetting. I only got on with Chermaine.' Elizabeth also admits, 'I'm going to miss her,' but adds that 'the last week has been difficult.' With Chermaine gone, the girls go for a much-needed weekend away and return in sombre mood. Jenny sums their feelings up: 'It's one less person to compete against, but it's still crap she left.'

With the mood in the flat still low, the girls are excited to hear they are going to a *Flux Magazine* party. Despite themselves, they actually have loads of fun getting ready and really enjoy the evening. Work also seems to be picking up and Jenny has been asked to do a shoot in Ireland for a leading department store. All four girls go on a casting for a swimwear shoot but only Alicia and Elizabeth are chosen. The competition for work is hotting up, and the girls are

'Elizabeth has helped me get through the past few weeks. She makes me laugh so much.' *Alicia*

about to do a photoshoot for *Cosmopolitan* which will reunite them with Chermaine and Maisie and the other finalists. The girls are overjoyed to see each other again, but the four remaining finalists know it's only a matter of time before two of them are rejected...

## Two Go Through

Four become two in the next stage of the *Model Behaviour* competition – each of the girls has been allowed to invite three members of their family or friends to a small party where the two finalists will be announced. 'We knew we were going down to two about a week before. On the day, everyone was quite nervous except me. I just decided to enjoy myself and have a laugh,' recalls Patricia. As well as family, the *MB* experts – Rafah, Gladeana and Maryon – were also there to meet the girls, possibly for the last time, and soak up the party atmosphere. The judges finally arrive to announce who will be going to London Fashion Week and be in with a fifty-fifty chance of becoming a *Cosmo* cover girl. 'The judges came at about 8.45pm and made us line up with our family behind us. They went to each of us in turn and did a recap on how well we'd done and what work we'd done,' recalls Elizabeth.

After all the build-up, Angus reveals the judges' decision: 'Unfortunately, we can only pick two people tonight and the first one is... Elizabeth. Congratulations on getting through to the next stage.' 'I was really happy and I hugged everyone,' recalls Elizabeth. Alicia was pleased for her friend too: 'I hugged her about 100 times that night. She cried and I had never seen her cry in all the time before.' 'I was really happy for her,' agrees Patricia. 'I really wanted her to get through because she really wanted it, she's a nice girl and she deserves it. I thought, "That's brilliant – it could only be better if it was me"' admits Jenny. But she and the others had to had to wait a bit longer, as she explains: 'The judges chatted and it seemed like forever and I was like, "Put us out of our misery!" I was so relieved when they said my name. Thank God!' Jenny was obviously ecstatic at the news, and Patricia swallowed her disappointment to congratulate her. 'When they said Jenny was the other one I was a bit upset but I went over and gave her a big hug. She didn't even get through the first ten initially, so I was pleased for her,' she says.

After much hilarity and hugs it was time for Alicia and Patricia to pack their bags and leave the *MB* flat for the final time... 'It was weird leaving. When I woke up in the morning at home it was a bit strange," remembers Patricia. Alicia claims she was glad she hadn't got through and pleased to be going home: 'I have never appreciated my life more than I do now I'm out. I am so tired – I've done nothing but sleep since I got back.' For Elizabeth and Jenny, life is about to get even more hectic as they prepare for London Fashion Week, where they will be appearing in their first professional catwalk show...

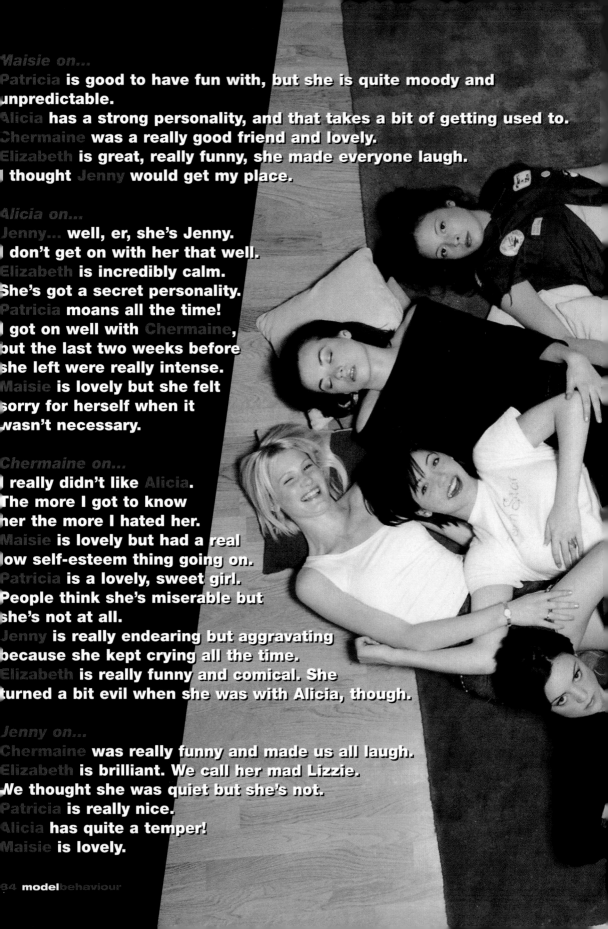

**Maisie on...**
**Patricia** is good to have fun with, but she is quite moody and unpredictable.
**Alicia** has a strong personality, and that takes a bit of getting used to.
**Chermaine** was a really good friend and lovely.
**Elizabeth** is great, really funny, she made everyone laugh.
I thought **Jenny** would get my place.

**Alicia on...**
**Jenny**... well, er, she's Jenny.
I don't get on with her that well.
**Elizabeth** is incredibly calm.
She's got a secret personality.
**Patricia** moans all the time!
I got on well with **Chermaine**, but the last two weeks before she left were really intense.
**Maisie** is lovely but she felt sorry for herself when it wasn't necessary.

**Chermaine on...**
I really didn't like **Alicia**.
The more I got to know her the more I hated her.
**Maisie** is lovely but had a real low self-esteem thing going on.
**Patricia** is a lovely, sweet girl. People think she's miserable but she's not at all.
**Jenny** is really endearing but aggravating because she kept crying all the time.
**Elizabeth** is really funny and comical. She turned a bit evil when she was with Alicia, though.

**Jenny on...**
**Chermaine** was really funny and made us all laugh.
**Elizabeth** is brilliant. We call her mad Lizzie. We thought she was quiet but she's not.
**Patricia** is really nice.
**Alicia** has quite a temper!
**Maisie** is lovely.

# girl *on* girl

**Elizabeth on...**

Alicia and me get on really well. We just understand each other I think.
I like Jenny, She's really sweet and giggly.
Chermaine is great to be with.
I like Tricia because she's cool and relaxed, except early in the morning.
I will definitely stay in contact with Maisie – we have a lot in common.

**Patricia on...**

Maisie was always putting herself down – I hated that, I would tell her to shut-up.
Jenny moans a lot but is very sweet.
I really only got on with Chermaine.
Nothing is ever good enough for Alicia.
Elizabeth never complains – she's very calm and she's really mad.

# life on the
# catwalk

For every successful model, there are thousands of wannabes. And of those who are successful, only a tiny proportion will become famous supermodels with bank balances to match. For the rest, modelling is very much a job like any other. It's hard work to ensure you stay on top. Cover girls may get to wear great clothes, sport fantastic make-up and travel the world, but they soon get sick of seeing the inside of airports and hotel bedrooms, having eyelids like cast iron, and changing outfits more often than Jennifer Lopez. Still, sunrise on a tropical Jamaican beach sounds rather more fun than a bleak, dreary Monday on the 7.13am to Paddington to me!

New talent enters the fashion industry daily. It's a competitive world and no matter how famous and beautiful a model is she has to cope with rejection throughout her career. Trends change too: what's in vogue this year may be out of style next, and that includes a model's 'look'. So, if modelling isn't about glamorous locations, celebrity friends and star-studded parties – what is it really like?

## new faces

Novice models may get a shock to discover that life on the catwalk can be extremely draining and very boring, as the *Model Behaviour* finalists discovered for themselves. 'It's not as exciting and glamorous as people might think, being a model,' says Alicia. 'I think unless you are naturally very good in front of the camera, mentally it's very, very difficult.'

You may be on top of the world to hear you've just been signed to an agency... but this is where the hard work really begins. First off, you'll need a portfolio and this is where the agency can really help get your career kick-started. All models have to have a test shoot to determine whether their beauty transforms into print. It's no good being attractive if you look like the back end of a bus in photographs. Test shoots give a new model experience of a studio situation, get them used to having their hair and make-up done and enable the agency to see how they cope with being the centre of attention. The agency will select a photographer and stylists to give the model a complete make-over before the shoot.

The ten *Model Behaviour* girls selected to complete the Workshop Week were treated to having a make-over with the help of stylist Charty Durrant, owner of Toni & Guy Anthony Mascolo, make-up artist Mark Cook and fashion photographer Donna Francesca. The girls were then given lessons on how to walk the catwalk by the famous Jay Alexander. In the real world, fledgling models are not given the five-star treatment and have to learn the art of looking good and walking tall on the job, as Premier Model Management's Head Booker Angus Munro explains: 'We never groom anybody as such, or train them to walk on a catwalk. We may have their hair cut, but essentially we get them ready, get them tested and send them out with their book.'

Once you have your set of test shoots for your portfolio, it's time for a whirlwind of go-sees and castings, where you only have a few seconds to make a good impression. First impressions last, and this is your chance to shine. 'Castings are just five seconds in and out,' reveals Alicia. Photographer Donna Francesca has worked for numerous fashion magazines including *Vogue*, *Elle* and *Harpers & Queen* and sits on the other side of the castings fence. 'Doing the castings can be quite disconcerting for both sides,' she explains. 'There's a classic line at go-sees – "Thanks for coming by" – which usually means "Thank you, I'm not interested." If you like them you may use the line too but you tend to chat and find out what they like and dislike. Personality is very important.'

Models also need to know how to walk down the catwalk too – and it isn't as easy as they make it look. 'Having to learn to walk on the catwalk was probably the most nerve-racking thing I've had to do. I hated it, though it was good learning to do it properly,' admits Patricia. Elizabeth confesses that 'walking' is not her best point: 'After I was picked, the first thing Angus said was that I was terrible on the catwalk.'

Attending castings and go-sees is an integral part of becoming a model. You may go to as many as ten 'go-sees' in a day and they may be spread across a wide area. Which means you'll be traipsing the streets, getting lost and standing around with hordes of other young hopefuls waiting to be seen. That can be depressing. 'You go to a lot of castings and you'll be told they don't want you for most of them,' Jenny explains. 'I wasn't expecting limos or anything but castings only last about thirty seconds. You can travel up to an hour to go see this person and in a few seconds that'll be it. That was very strange at first,' she muses. Each meeting brings its own rush of nerves and chance of rejection… but you have to remain cheerful and let your personality shine through, as judge Lorraine Candy points out: 'If I see two girls at a shoot who are both stunningly beautiful, and one's got a fabulous personality we'll choose her.' Each client looks for something unique and individual in every model. So if you're not chosen this time, it may be your turn next.

## landing a job

That first assignment is a model's dream – it's what she's been preparing for since she embarked on her journey to be a cover girl. Fashion shows can be gruelling affairs that really test a model's stamina. Doing collections can be so overwhelming that models get emotionally and physically drained. Do you think you could handle up to five shows a day, rehearsals, fittings and actually doing the catwalk modelling? Fashion photo shoots can be just as tiring too. You'll be constantly primped and preened, on your feet for several hours and ready to pose for hours at a time. If you're on location that could mean leisurely shoots by the sea or it could mean

1. **WALK TALL** The way you carry yourself tells a client a lot about you. Stand tall and don't slouch.
2. **STAY CALM** Learn to cope with nerves. Practise relaxation techniques to keep your cool.
3. **USE YOUR BRAIN** Ask questions if you don't understand and make sure you pay attention to what's being said.
4. **DON'T BITCH** It's a small industry. Bad-mouthing clients, agents and other models won't do you any favours.
5. **KEEP SMILING** Remember, this could be your big break, so be happy and look like you are enjoying yourself.
6. **BE PUNCTUAL** Arriving five minutes early will show you're professional; arriving five minutes late will tell a different story.
7. **BE ENGAGING** Be prepared to chat about things that interest you.
8. **DRESS SIMPLY** Prospective clients want to see the natural you. A subtle individual touch, like an interesting belt or shoes, will help make an impression.
9. **KEEP NATURAL** Don't overdo your make-up. Keep it minimal and simple to accentuate your natural beauty.
10. **LOOK 'EM IN THE EYE** Make eye-to-eye contact to show you are interested.

posing in a Merino wool suit in 35-degree sunshine. Could you handle five hours posing in a bikini in 10-degree temperatures and driving rain? You need infinite patience to be a model. Ask yourself – have you really got what it takes to last the course?

## manage your money

You must be the type of person that can use your own initiative and manage your own life and finances properly. Handling money is a vital skill for life, not just modelling. Are you the kinda girl that blows your first pay cheque on a Prada handbag when you've no food in the fridge, or do you sensibly put money aside for a rainy day? The *Model Behaviour* chaperone Rafah Sabbagh believes, 'The girls will certainly have to centre themselves financially if they go on to model professionally.' A model's career is generally a short one; it pays to invest your money wisely, so you have something left over when the work finally dries up.

## stay safe

Trudging the streets of a foreign city may be exciting, but it can be dangerous too. Keep yourself safe by being sensible and following these golden rules:

> **'Models have to get used to a lot of people telling them that they don't have the right look. That's a tough thing to deal with. Keep an open mind and don't let things that people say to you get you down too much.'**
> *Oliver Woods, Judge*

1. Never give out your home address or landline to scouts or prospective clients.
2. If you are suspicious about a booking, cancel it.
3. Don't hand over money to an agency before signing a contract.
4. Don't shell out dosh to have professional shots done – go to see some agencies first.
5. If you are under eighteen, make sure your parents are involved in visiting agencies and castings.
6. If you are approached by someone who claims to be a scout, ask for their card and phone the agency they work for first before giving out personal details.
7. Take a friend with you to go-sees and auditions.
8. If you travel by cab, always use a licensed taxi.
9. Carry your keys in your hand – keys can be an effective weapon if the need arises.
10. Don't walk around in dark, unlit areas on your own. And take a map so you don't get lost.

## coping with rejection

Don't get downcast when you aren't picked. It takes time to establish a career in the fashion business. Talk to others in the industry for guidance and advice and give yourself time. Rejection comes with the territory and it's something you have to get used to. Claudia Schiffer was rejected by a number of agencies before she finally landed a contract – and look at her now!

The fashion business is a real ego-bruiser, so you need strong self-esteem. You'll be judged over and over again on how you look, and invariably be told you are not what the client wants. 'Models are generally mature and pretty tough because they get rejected several times a day,' points out *Cosmopolitan* Editor, Lorraine Candy. Patricia reckons it takes a certain inner strength to cope, 'I think if they like me they like me and if they don't they don't. I don't really care.' Are you hard enough to take repeated knocks, or will you fall to pieces? 'Criticism doesn't bother me,' says Elizabeth, 'I know what I'm like and my friends and family know what I'm like. At the end of the day that's all that matters.' If you are determined to model, make sure you have something to fall back on and that you have other interests to stimulate you, to help you cope with rejection and waiting for that first job.

## keeping your options open

It is wise to have a back-up plan in case you find you are not model girl material. If you are studying for GCSEs or A Levels, make sure you stay with the course. It's sensible to get some qualifications under your belt — even if you are a success there will come a time when you get too old to model and need to turn your attentions to something else. Savvy cover girls such as Elle MacPherson have used their business acumen and brains to carve out a whole new

**'Eat well. Live well. Don't worry about your weight and being pencil thin.'** *Rafah Sabbagh, Chaperone*

career. And, if things don't work out quite as you planned, at least you then have other options to explore. Premier's Angus Munro agrees: 'We would never tell a girl at school to drop out to be a model. We would advise them to do modelling part-time and finish their studies. If it doesn't work out, they've then got something to fall back on. We wouldn't normally sign a girl who is under sixteen. Your face changes between sixteen and eighteen, so the average age is probably seventeen to eighteen.'

Don't feel you might miss out on your chance to become a cover girl if you stay at school either — any decent model agency will respect your wishes and encourage you to finish your education and model part-time. As *Model Behaviour* finalist Maisie reveals, 'I wanted to be successful as a model [though] now I know I can't. But at least I have tried. If I had got through I still would have finished my A Levels.'

## learn to let go

If you don't find success after giving it your best shot, don't be afraid to quit. Modelling doesn't suit everyone and it takes a brave person to admit it isn't for them, and find something more fulfilling to do instead. Remember — most models' careers, rather like those of footballers, are short-lived, so it's definitely worth training for another vocation while you are trying to cut it as a cover girl. Life coach Gladeana McMahon points out that: 'Modelling is a time-limited career, so you must be someone that looks ahead and doesn't just live from day-to-day. You need to think about where you want to be in five or ten years' time.'

If you are dead-set on working in the fashion industry, there are lots of other career opportunities to consider, such as fashion designer, make-up artist, hair stylist, PR and photographer. Learn to deal with your successes and your failures and most of all, enjoy yourself whatever you do with your life. Good luck!

**'You don't become a model overnight. It takes experience and you must look after yourself, because at the end of the day it's what you put into it that you get out of it.'** *Mark Cook, Make-up artist*

# cover *girls*

## London Fashion Week

It's Sunday, and disaster has struck as Jenny is in bed with flu. 'I feel awful and I keep losing my voice,' she croaks. She decides to stay in bed in the hope that she will feel better tomorrow – the first day of London Fashion Week, one of the biggest events on a model's calendar.

Monday morning dawns and Jenny still feels rough. 'I woke up and I couldn't move. I couldn't get out of bed,' she wails. Nevertheless, she is determined to appear in LFW whatever: 'I forced myself out of bed and said to myself, "I'm going to do this. Unless I collapse,

I'm going to do this."' While Jenny prepares to get up from her sick bed, Elizabeth decides to go on ahead and take in a couple of shows: 'I was really excited about going to the shows so I went to watch one this morning and met up with Jenny after lunch for a rehearsal. It was very strange doing the shows, Lady Victoria Hervey was modelling too.'

Arriving dosed up for her flu, Jenny finds her first show very nerve-wracking: 'Elizabeth and I did the Robert Cary-Williams show today, which was really weird because we didn't have time for a rehearsal. The shoes I had to wear were size 7 and I'm size 5 and they had five inch heels so I was like "Oh my God."' Tuesday saw the girls taking part in the Michiko Koshino show and both Elizabeth and Jenny were calmer by then as Jenny recalls, 'By the second show I kinda knew what I was doing.'

Jenny is clearly enjoying herself by her third show. 'On the John Rocha show I got to walk out with the designer at the end – that was brilliant. He said I should come back next year,' she gushes. The girls then put on their party gear, and were whisked away to the Premier party, to let their hair down and have a good time.

Elizabeth and Jenny waiting to model Robert Cary-Williams' collection.

Next day, the girls have the chance to watch some shows and check out the celebrities in the audience. 'I saw Samantha Mumba, *Big Brother*'s Narinder and Brian, and Boy George,' reveals Elizabeth. Then it's Elizabeth's turn to travel across London for a shoot for *Flux Magazine*, leaving Jenny to take in more catwalk action. Both girls are pleasantly surprised at how much they've enjoyed doing catwalk shows... 'I always thought I wanted to do photographic modelling rather than fashion but now I've done catwalk it gives you such a buzz and it's really, really good. I imagined it to be a whole big ball of scariness and it's not that at all. It's such a good buzz,' says Jenny. Elizabeth agrees, 'It was a big thrill to do the shows in London Fashion Week.

As well as enjoying the shows, the girls learned a lot too. 'When you're walking down the catwalk you don't want to concentrate too hard because it makes your walk look silly, but you do have to think about what you are going to do at the end and whether you're in the right spot on the catwalk,' explains Elizabeth. Elizabeth found the catwalk difficult but she's surprised herself: 'My walk has improved. We met up with Jay Alexander the other day and he says it's much

better since he last saw us.' Jenny soon got used to the flashing cameras too: 'It was really weird walking down the catwalk and seeing about 200 cameras pointing at your face. I had to just focus on a head or something and put my eyes in a daze so I didn't get distracted.'

On Thursday, Elizabeth gets ready backstage to take part in the Richard Kinloch show, with Jenny in the audience. 'It's really busy backstage with racks of clothes and shoes everywhere and girls jumping in and out of outfits,' says Elizabeth. Next day both girls get the chance to view a couple of shows and pick up some tips from some well-established models. Despite competing against each other for the coveted first prize of a *Cosmo* cover and a year's contract with Premier, the girls are really supportive of each other and all rivalry is temporarily forgotten.

Elizabeth has finally heard she has been chosen by lingerie designer Damaris to model her new collection, after a casting over six weeks ago. 'The rooms were tiny and you had to walk from one to the other. People were right next to you so it was very strange. I wore a slip with holes in it and a denim skirt,' she recalls.

With London Fashion Week over, the girls go home for the weekend for a much needed rest, but have to be back in the *MB* apartment by Sunday evening ready for the *Cosmopolitan* cover shoot the next day.

## Cover Girls

It's nine o'clock on Monday morning and the girls arrive at The Works Studio in West London, where the *Cosmopolitan* cover shoot is taking place. Both girls will be photographed, though only one will ultimately be used on the cover. 'They told us to get plenty of sleep over the weekend. I went to a party Saturday night and didn't go to bed until 5.00am. Sunday I didn't get back to the flat until 11.00pm,' confesses Elizabeth. But she's still looking good despite suffering with a bad cold.

*Cosmo* Fashion Editor Caroline Baxter, make-up artist Dani Guinsburg and hair stylist Allison McKay then get to work transforming Elizabeth and Jenny into glamorous cover girls. A *Cosmo* model has to have a certain look, as Editor-in-Chief and *Model Behaviour* judge Lorraine Candy explains: 'A cover girl must be really sexy, really fresh, really modern and very glamorous, but not edgy. Being a *Cosmo* girl is about being happy.' Both Elizabeth and Jenny are very relaxed about the shoot, with no sign of nerves until Lorraine sits them down to remind them just how important today is. 'Do you realise that today I'm putting my job on the line?' she asks. 'I'm going to shoot pictures of both of you, and one of those will be on the front cover of *Cosmopolitan*. This is the culmination of everything you have

> **'Magazines make the models. Once they get a cover shoot that is what raises their profile and then they become famous.'**
> *Lorraine Candy, Judge*

learnt over the last few months, and you must rise to the challenge. You have to work hard today and get me a good front cover because if you don't, there is a good chance you're not going to win.' Both Jenny and Elizabeth are now more anxious about the shoot and are aware that they will have to give it all they've got if they are to claim the ultimate prize. Jenny in particular is worried because she knows Lorraine isn't sure she's a *Cosmo* girl, but Lorraine is keeping an open mind, and at the end of the day

personality counts as much as looks: 'Most of the girls who we get in for cover shoots are a joy to be with and we have a great time and that comes through in the photo. Personality is very important.'

With their make-up and hair done, the girls put on the first set of clothes – Jenny an orange top and white trousers, and Elizabeth a very feminine floral dress. 'It went well at the *Cosmo* shoot. I was made to look glamorous and not so edgy,' recalls Jenny. The shoot lasts well into the evening as the girls are shot in different outfits and poses. By 7.30pm Lorraine, Kate Elkin the Art Director, and photographer Carlo Dalla Chiesa were satisfied with the Polaroids – one of the girls would be suitable for the December issue of *Cosmopolitan*... but which one? 'I still don't know who will win because we both looked good,' says Jenny. 'Once I had seen the Polaroids I could see both Elizabeth and I working on the cover. I didn't look too weird and I thought maybe I was back in with a chance.' The girls still have nearly two weeks to wait before the winner is announced...

Since both girls have made it this far, neither is admitting that winning is important. 'I am really positive and I have been all the way through. I won't be too upset if I don't win. If I win a contract with Premier it will have to be part-time. I'm taking GCSE's this summer,' says Elizabeth. Jenny feels much the same way: 'Now it's not major if I don't win. I'd be happy if Elizabeth won and happy if I did.' But deep down, they do care. 'Ultimately I'll be a little disappointed if I don't win because it would be really, really brilliant, but I'll be happy for Elizabeth if she wins,' confesses Jenny.

## Trip of a Lifetime

The girls are informed that they are about to be whisked away to a secret destination abroad for a final photoshoot for *Cosmopolitan*. Neither Jenny nor Elizabeth has travelled much before, so they are understandably excited. 'We were told to meet at Heathrow and then we were told we were flying to Iceland!' explains Jenny. On arriving at the hotel in Reykjavik the girls go out to dinner and retire to bed early ready for the busy day ahead. The girls have less than a week left to impress the judges – the final winner will be announced just five days after they return from Iceland.

The shoot takes place 1,400 metres up a mountain at sub-zero temperatures, so the girls will be tested to the limit. 'We drove six hours up a glacier to do the shoot. It was amazing,' recalls Jenny. It's snowing but the light is perfect so the crew and Lorraine are feeling confident... circumstances change rapidly, however, as the weather begins to turn and the trucks can't get through the snow. After abandoning the trailer (along with all the equipment and clothes) at the bottom of the mountain, the team continue their journey by snowmobile. 'We had to wait an hour for the gear to be ferried up by snowmobile before we could get started on the photo session,' recalls Justin Gorman, the show's Series Producer.' 'I was shouting, "Where the hell are the clothes?"' recalls Lorraine.

With the pressure mounting and Lorraine getting increasingly anxious about the failing light, Elizabeth and Jenny start getting into their clothes. 'In my first shot I wore a dress, brown fur coat and a hat. I had to lay in the snow which was absolutely freezing,' recalls Jenny. Several hours later, the girls had proved how well they could do in difficult conditions and under pressure, and Lorraine is pleased with the final pictures. After a hard day's work the girls take a snowmobile ride down the mountain, a trip they'll never forget. 'It was amazing!' enthuses Jenny. 'It was great fun but they wouldn't let me drive it!' jokes Elizabeth.

It's day three in Iceland, and Elizabeth and Jenny go to a health spa called the Blue Lagoon, a thermal geological lake where the water is so hot it steams. 'I put on a bikini and dressing gown and I was absolutely freezing standing on the side. When I got into the water it was like swimming in a kettle. It was boiling. I had to keep getting out to cool down,' recalls Jenny. Elizabeth was a bit put out when she wasn't allowed in because the stylists didn't want her to ruin her hair, but they soon relented. 'It was brilliant but I had to swim around while trying to keep my head completely out of the water,' she says. Then, after a photo session on the lava fields, the girls return to the hotel and an early night in preparation for their last day in Iceland. 'We went sight-seeing on Friday to the geysers and then we went shopping. Reykjavik has loads of expensive designer shops,' Elizabeth remembers.

## The Final Verdict

After flying back from Iceland it's time to leave the *Model Behaviour* flat for the last time. Jenny and Elizabeth pack up their belongings and make the jour-ney home. 'I am really worried about going back to school on Monday,' confesses Elizabeth. Jenny is anxious too: 'It's really strange to be going. We've been here for ages and it's like we're being kicked out of the nest. It's going to be quite difficult to readjust to life at home.' The girls can't wait until Saturday to find out the result of the competition. 'I'm looking forward to getting told who has won,' says Elizabeth, 'I have no idea where my life's taking me after Saturday.' Jenny too wants to get it over with: 'I am now a little bit nerv-ous about the final stage.'

While the two finalists wait anxiously, the judges meet to make their final decision. Angus, Lorraine and Ollie watch endless video clips of the two girls and scrutinise all the pictures produced for their model books. Lorraine has always seen Elizabeth as a *Cosmo* girl and admits she originally didn't think Jenny could ever appear on the cover. However, after working with her in Iceland and on the cover shoot, she has changed her mind, which means Jenny is now in with a real chance. Angus makes no secret that he has always favoured Jenny because of her distinctive look, but he takes into account the fact that Elizabeth is only sixteen and has done really well to get this far. Ollie can see potential in both finalists and likes both their looks. Which one will they choose? After a full day of hammering it out, they come to a final verdict, but it's a close run thing...

Saturday dawns and Jenny and Elizabeth are driven to a restaurant in West London, where the winner will be announced. Both sets of families are there for support. 'We got to the pub and had lunch though me and Jenny didn't eat much. After lunch, Jenny and I were chatting for ages and agreed we'd

both won in a way. We both saw it right through. We both hoped we would get what we wanted out of this,' reveals Elizabeth. After the meal, the room is cleared and Elizabeth and Jenny wait with their families.

'The judges arrived and told Elizabeth and I in turn how we'd done so far,' explains Jenny. Elizabeth remem-bers the final moments very clearly: 'They said they were worried at the start because they thought I was shy and that I had a terrible walk, but now they realise I'm not shy and my walk has improved. Then they went to Jenny and said despite not getting picked as one of the five she had worked really hard to get this far.'

The judges explained how difficult it has been to choose one girl over the other. 'After much deliberation, we have decided that Jenny is the winner,' reveals Angus. 'Elizabeth has all the attributes a model would need, albeit she is a little young and her face isn't fully developed. She has the height, she has the figure, and she has good hair. Jenny came in late and worked extremely well – better than the others – the competi-tion was about how hard they've tried and how they've come through the ranks and how much they worked. That's why Jenny was chosen.'

Jenny screams and jumps up and down for joy: 'I am ecstatic about winning. I didn't expect it at all. I couldn't believe it. I got squashed and squeezed by my whole family. I was just in a state of shock. I was too happy and shocked to cry. I was like, "Oh my God, I'm going to be a model for a year and be on the cover of *Cosmopolitan*."' Elizabeth was stunned too: 'Everyone started clapping. I felt quite shaky and at that point I felt I didn't want to go back to school – I wanted to be a model. Jenny's family came over and congratulated me.'

'I went and gave Elizabeth a cuddle and I felt bad for her because only one of us could win. She didn't seem too upset, but she did say she didn't want to do her GCSE's now and that she wanted to be a model. It was probably the moment and I'm sure she'll return to that,' recalls a triumphant Jenny. 'It's really strange. I never thought I had a chance of winning because they didn't pick me to be one of the five. It's like I was a reject and I wasn't right for *Cosmopolitan* because I had an edgy look. It surprised Lorraine, I think; that once I had my hair and make-up done I actually turned out quite pretty on the photos.' Lorraine admits Jenny wasn't her first choice initially, but she was won over by her personality: 'Jenny has an amazing look, but not one I'd normally use in *Cosmo*. One of the reasons we picked her was because we knew she was working. The essence of *Cosmo* is this "can-do, overcome everything, get what you want if you really, really want it" attitude. Jenny's personality really exemplifies that. I've never seen anyone be so professional, work so hard and want something so much. I felt she so deserved it. It was real proof that personality is as important as looks.'

'I was a little disappointed not to win,' confesses Elizabeth. 'The judges said they spent a whole day deciding and kept changing their minds. So I was a winner at one point. I'm fine about it now.'

The following week, Jenny heads up to London to Premier Model Management to sign her contract for a year. It's the agency that launched Naomi Campbell and Claudia Schiffer on the road to model superstardom. Will it do the same for her? 'I think that anybody we take on for a year does have the chance of becoming a big name model. It really depends on who picks them up. It is very possible Jenny will do well,' says Angus.

As Elizabeth returns to school, she has a busy year ahead of her, studying for her GCSE's. Jenny moves into Premier's real-life model's apartment in London to launch her modelling career full-time. Already, things are looking promising as she has been booked to appear in *Vogue* and has even been called in for a casting by legendary fashion photographer Mario Testino, an amazing achievement for a girl who has only been modelling for five weeks. As she goes to see *Cosmopolitan* run off the presses at the printers, she still can't believe it: 'Oh my God, it's me on the cover. That's absolutely amazing.' It won't be long before Jenny is one of the most recognized models in Britain, and all thanks to *Model Behaviour* and Jenny's determination to make it in the busi- ness. For a single mum struggling to bring up her daughter in a small town in Wales, the opportunity to become a model is a dream come true. 'I have always wanted to be a model. I have never ever wanted anything else and it's like I've achieved my ambition,' smiles Jenny. It seems that some dreams really do come true...

**'Jenny really, really wanted it so I'm happy for her.'** *Elizabeth*

'I'm chuffed to bits to have won. I'm still in shock.' *Jenny*